P9-CEG-616

Spontaneous Melodramas

24 impromptu skits that bring Bible stories to life

Spontaneous Melodramas

24 impromptu skits that bring Bible stories to life

Doug Fields

Laurie Polich

Duffy Robbins

Youth Specialties

ZondervanPublishingHouse
Grand Rapids, Michigan
A Division of HarperCollinsPublishers

Spontaneous Melodramas: 24 Impromptu Skits That Bring Bible Stories to Life
Copyright © 1996 by Youth Specialties, Inc.

Youth Specialties Books, 1224 Greenfield Dr., El Cajon, CA 92021, are published by Zondervan Publishing House, 5300 Patterson S.E., Grand Rapids, MI 49530.

Library of Congress Cataloging-in-Publication Data

Fields, Doug, 1962-
    Spontaneous melodramas: 24 impromptu skits that bring Bible stories to life/
Doug Fields, Laurie Polich, and Duffy Robbins.
        p.   cm.
    ISBN 0-310-20775
        1. Drama in Christian education.   2. Church work with youth.   3. Bible plays, American.
4. Christian drama, American.   5. Children's plays, American.
I. Polich, Laurie. II. Robbins, Duffy. III. Title.
BV1534.4.F54 1996
268'.67—dc20

95-48256
CIP

Unless otherwise indicated, all Scripture quotations are taken from the *Holy Bible: New International Version (North American Edition)*. Copyright © 1973, 1978, 1984 by the International Bible Society. Used by permission of Zondervan Bible Publishers.

The material in this book may be photocopied for local use in churches, youth groups, and other Christian education activities. Special permission is not necessary. However, the contents of this book may not be reproduced in any other form without written permission from the publisher. All rights reserved.

Edited by Joan Brasher and Tim McLaughlin
Cover and interior design by Patton Brothers Design

Printed in the United States of America

96 97 98 99 /   / 6 5 4 3 2 1

Table of contents

90970

What are spontaneous melodramas, anyway?

Spontaneous melodramas are exciting and creative ways to get students moving around, learning, and laughing while learning stories from God's Word. We've just never heard kids complain (*"That's so boring"*) after doing melodramas like these with them.

Melodramas get students involved in your lessons—and, given a biblical text, can make Bible studies come to life. It's no secret that students retain more when they're actively involved in the learning process. These melodramas can engage your students in active Bible study—not by merely hearing it or reading it, but by *doing* it!

Simply put, a spontaneous melodrama is a **humorous narrative reading**, during which actors dramatize the narrative's action—with **melodramatic exaggeration**, and **on the spot**, with **no rehearsals**.

It looks like this: you call the requisite number of teenagers up front, assign them their roles—animate or inanimate—and instruct them to do whatever you read. If you read that the trees wave furiously in gale-force winds, then the student trees do their best to wave furiously. If the protagonist is said to weep buckets, the student actor wails loudly—and the more melodramatic, the better.

Such overacting won't score with their high school drama instructor, but it's hilarious in a slapstick sort of way. Plus it makes the meeting—and the Bible story—memorable.

On the other hand, you know your kids and your own ministry context. So be discriminating about when a spontaneous melodrama is appropriate, about which one of these 24 are most suitable to your plans, about how you should adapt the melodrama to fit your group.

The melodramas in this book convey the message of the text in a fresh, creative, and occasionally goofy way. Yet they are still learning experiences that, however goofy, retain the central message of the Bible stories and help students visualize the passages as you teach them later. In fact, to make it easy for you to flow from the Bible passage to our melodramatic version of it (or vice versa), we've included the literal Bible text at the head of each of the twenty-four readings—because the point of these spontaneous melodramas is not their potential to bring down the house with overacted hilarity (though that's a close second), but their capacity to prod students to encounter the biblical text.

Take these spontaneous melodramas with you on a retreat. Use them on Sunday morning. Let them introduce your lesson on one of the classic Bible stories from the Old Testament (the Tower of Babel, Lot's wife, Joseph's dreams, Samson, Daniel, Jonah) or New Testament (the temptations of Jesus, the parables of the Good Samaritan and the Prodigal Son, the cleansing of the Temple). After all, if your kids are afflicted with some degree of biblical illiteracy, you can't assume they're familiar with these classics.

So with these two dozen melodramas, get your kids laughing—then get them learning.

Here's what we've learned leading youth groups in spontaneous melodramas:

✳ Add some planning to the spontaneity.

"Planned spontaneity"? Well, yes, kind of. A little preparation is quality control for your otherwise spontaneous production. In fact, at the beginning of each script are leader hints, which are suggestions we've found useful for performing that melodrama.

The *timing* of your reading and *casting* are everything. About timing: the humor can take a completely different turn (or drop out altogether) with different timing and delivery of a line. So be sure to read the melodrama through at least once before performing it, looking for places in the script which need your particular attention—where you can make or break the line.

As far as casting goes, select kids with personalities that will enhance the roles. Some very general suggestions are implicit in the cast lists at the beginning of each script. Just be careful and use your discernment: you don't want a student with a weight problem playing the part of a whale. Enough said.

❋ Mind your pauses and cues.

When a line you read calls for action, pause long enough for the actor(s) to act. No need to race through the scripts. Take your time!

❋ Tweak the scripts.

If the script calls for ten people and you have only five, rewrite it. Have students play more than one role. Not enough males in your group for a melodrama? Go ahead and use females. Alter the scripts however it best suits your group. Take all the poetic license you want in the narration, for a spontaneous melodrama's narration is as crucial as its acting.

Season your reading with impromptu comments and fillers. For example, if your actor doesn't deliver a line with sufficient enthusiasm, say something like "...and because Trueheart said his words so apathetically, the audience booed him until he spoke with conviction and enthusiasm." Is his delivery *still* lackluster? "...Finally, with the audience silent as snow, Trueheart screamed the words as if all the world could hear them..."

Or if this or that action or gesture is a big hit, capitalize on it by adding impromptu: "She kept dancing in circles while the audience counted to five."

Or if your bench or boat or boulder gets the giggles: "And the tree jumped from behind the bush and covered Jeanette's mouth so the audience could hear the rest of this melodrama."

You get the idea.

❋ Make it big.

The bigger, the broader, the more hyperbolic the action, the better. Get your kids thinking big falls, rubber faces, oversized movements and loud-loud-loud exclamations. Encourage your students to go all-out! They'll have more fun doing it—and everyone will have more fun watching it.

❋ Beware: these melodramas ain't mellow.

We admit it: now and then in these scripts you'll find isolated, infrequent instances of gratuitious nose-pickings and hand-in-armpit noises. On the other hand, it doesn't take an M.Div. to conclude that such spontaneous melodramas probably aren't appropriate for Sunday morning worship services. So change what you must to suit your group; you know the written and unwritten guidelines of taste in your church or youth group.

Furthermore, these are action scripts. Not much subtlety here. So you may want to rearrange your room some to allow for the action—especially since even the audience plays an active role in many of the scripts. After all, your goal is to get as many people as possible involved. And when you do a spontaneous melodrama, you may want to warn the Twilighters, the toddlers, or whatever Sunday school class is next door to the youth room: it may get a little, ah, boisterous.

Then again, they're probably used to it by now. ❋

The First Tongue Twister

Bible text

¹Now the whole world had one language and a common speech. ²As men moved eastward, they found a plain in Shinar and settled there.

³They said to each other, "Come, let's make bricks and bake them thoroughly." They used brick instead of stone, and tar for mortar. ⁴Then they said, "Come, let us build ourselves a city, with a tower that reaches to the heavens, so that we may make a name for ourselves and not be scattered over the face of the whole earth."

⁵But the Lord came down to see the city and the tower that the men were building. ⁶The Lord said, "If as one people speaking the same language they have begun to do this, then nothing they plan to do will be impossible for them. ⁷Come, let us go down and confuse their language so they will not understand each other."

⁸So the Lord scattered them from there over all the earth, and they stopped building the city. ⁹That is why it was called Babel — because there the Lord confused the language of the whole world. From there the Lord scattered them over the face of the whole earth.

Cast

* Rankara (male or female)
* Noistrata (male)
* Schmelda (female)
* The people of the world (3 or more)
* Blocks (6, females and males)
* Surfboard (female)

Props

* Playing cards
* Sign with HEAP written on it

Leader hints

This melodrama can use a little rehearsal, if there's time before the performance—specifically, the chant that Rankara, Noistrata, and Schmelda do together. By the way, about these three names—if you want, change them to whatever three names will entertain your group: local celebrities, presidential candidates if you live in New Hampshire or Iowa, three of the kids' favorite adult volunteers, etc. Toward the end of the script, read the surfer and jive lines with a normal voice—and let the students ham up the inflections.

As the scene opens...

The three people are onstage, and the six blocks are lying on top of one student, who is wearing the HEAP sign that isn't seen until the blocks are removed from the heap pile.

The book of Genesis, chapter eleven verse one, says: Now the whole world had one language and a common speech. Few people know that that language was Pig Latin. As the people of the world moved east across the desert plain, Rankara said in his native tongue, "Ets lay iv lay ite ray ere hay!"

Noistrata said, "Oh nay a way oo yay ishful way eamer dray!"

Schmelda said, "Let's stop this Pig Latin thing or this is going to be the longest and most confusing melodrama in the history of the world, and the world was just created ten chapters ago."

The crowd cheered because they were totally confused.

Rankara was happy to start over and said in English, "Let's live right here!"

Noistrata said, "No way."

Schmelda said, "Way! This place is cool!"

So they settled right on that very spot. They did nothing all day except sit in the sun and play Go Fish.

Rankara said to Schmelda, "Got any fives?"

Schmelda said, "Go fish."

Noistrata said to Rankara, "Got any threes?"

Rankara said, "Go fish."

The audience knew what a long and stupid game this was so they fell asleep and made loud, long, and obnoxious snoring sounds.

Noistrata said, "This is getting a little boring."

Rankara said, "We deserve a break today."

"Yeah," said Noistrata. "Sometimes you gotta break the rules."

"Have it your way," said Schmelda.

"We need the real thing," said Rankara.

"Yeah, we're a new generation," said Noistrata.

"Obey your thirst," said Schmelda.

The world's people put their heads together and concocted a plan. They decided to build a fabulous worship center on a nearby hill, using six blocks they found lying in a nearby heap. They pulled the blocks from the heap and dragged them to center stage. The crowd gave the heap a nice applause for agreeing to volunteer for a role that is basically meaningless.

The world's people then arranged the blocks to form a pyramid that reached all the way to the sky.

"Now I really feel like a somebody," the people said in unison.

They pranced around their tower ten times chanting, "I ay ott gay ass gay," which is Pig Latin for "I got gas."

As the audience held their noses, the Lord looked down on this sorry situation. Frankly, he wasn't very happy. He said, "If as one people speaking the same language they have begun to do this, then who knows what depths they'll sink to?"

And he was right. Already the people were making gross hand-in-armpit noises, acting like dorks, and mimicking every Three Stooges stunt they could remember. Drastic measures had to be taken, the Lord decided—so he changed all their languages so they couldn't understand each other.

Rankara suddenly began speaking a language the others couldn't understand: "Dude, like, there's a lot of beach, but where are the waves?" Rankara threw a surfboard over her shoulder and headed west *(or east, if that's where your nearest surfing sites are)*.

Noistrata suddenly found himself speaking jive. Turning to Schmelda, he said, "Yo, baby, you lookin' mighty fine wich yo fresh threads."

Schmelda, not understanding, spoke back to him in sign language: she slapped him across the face.

And thus the various people groups of the world gained their own identities and headed off in their own directions. And gradually the tower eroded slowly to the ground, never to rise again. ✳

Death of Lot's wife, Genesis 19

A Salt with a Deadly Woman

Bible text

[1]The two angels arrived at Sodom in the evening, and Lot was sitting in the gateway of the city. When he saw them, he got up to meet them and bowed down with his face to the ground. [2]"My lords," he said, "please turn aside to your servant's house. You can wash your feet and spend the night and then go on your way early in the morning."

"No," they answered, "we will spend the night in the square."

[3]But he insisted so strongly that they did go with him and entered his house. He prepared a meal for them, baking bread without yeast, and they ate. [4]Before they had gone to bed, all the men from every part of the city of Sodom — both young and old — surrounded the house. [5]They called to Lot, "Where are the men who came to you tonight? Bring them out to us so that we can have sex with them."

[6]Lot went outside to meet them and shut the door behind him [7]and said, "No, my friends. Don't do this wicked thing. [8]Look, I have two daughters who have never slept with a man. Let me bring them out to you, and you can do what you like with them. But don't do anything to these men, for they have come under the protection of my roof."

[9]"Get out of our way," they replied. And they said, "This fellow came here as an alien, and now he wants to play the judge! We'll treat you worse than them." They kept bringing pressure on Lot and moved forward to break down the door.

[10]But the men inside reached out and pulled Lot back into the house and shut the door. [11]Then they struck the men who were at the door of the house, young and old, with blindness so that they could not find the door.

[12]The two men said to Lot, "Do you have anyone else here — sons-in-law, sons or daughters, or anyone else in the city who belongs to you? Get them out of here, [13]because we are going to destroy this place. The outcry to the Lord against its people is so great that he has sent us to destroy it."

[14]So Lot went out and spoke to his sons-in-law, who were pledged to marry his daughters. He said, "Hurry and get out of this place, because the Lord is about to destroy the city!" But his sons-in-law thought he was joking.

[15]With the coming of dawn, the angels urged Lot, saying, "Hurry! Take your wife and your two daughters who are here, or you will be swept away when the city is punished."

[16]When he hesitated, the men grasped his hand and the hands of his wife and of his two daughters and led them safely out of the city, for the Lord was merciful to them. [17]As soon as they had brought them out, one of them said, "Flee for your lives! Don't look back, and don't stop anywhere in the plain! Flee to the mountains or you will be swept away!"

[18]But Lot said to them, "No, my lords, please! [19]Your servant has found favor in your eyes, and you have shown great kindness to me in sparing my life. But I can't flee to the mountains; this disaster will overtake me, and I'll die. [20]Look, here is a town near enough to run to, and it is small. Let me flee to it—it is very small, isn't it? Then my life will be spared."

[21]He said to him, "Very well, I will grant this request too; I will not overthrow the town you speak of. [22]But flee there quickly, because I cannot do anything until you reach it." (That is why the town was called Zoar.)

23By the time Lot reached Zoar, the sun had risen over the land. 24Then the Lord rained down burning sulfur on Sodom and Gomorrah—from the Lord out of the heavens. 25Thus he overthrew those cities and the entire plain, including all those living in the cities—and also the vegetation in the land. 26But Lot's wife looked back, and she became a pillar of salt.

27Early the next morning Abraham got up and returned to the place where he had stood before the Lord. 28He looked down toward Sodom and Gomorrah, toward all the land of the plain, and he saw dense smoke rising from the land, like smoke from a furnace.

29So when God destroyed the cities of the plain, he remembered Abraham, and he brought Lot out of the catastrophe that overthrew the cities where Lot had lived.

30Lot and his two daughters left Zoar and settled in the mountains, for he was afraid to stay in Zoar. He and his two daughters lived in a cave.

Cast

* Lot
* Lot's wife
* Lot's two daughters
* Two angels (females or males)
* Citizens of Sodom and Gomorrah (2)
* Joe Friday
* Phone (a person who makes a ringing sound)
* Siren (can also be the Phone character)
* Theme music hummers (audience, which hums the old "Dragnet" theme: Dum, duh-dum-dum...Dum, duh-dum-dum DAA)
* Gate of the city (2 people, standing, facing each other, hands raised and joined over their heads.)
* Unruly mob (2 or 3, optional)

Props

* Salt
* Pipe (for Joe Friday — and, without tobacco , thank you)

Leader hints

Rehearse the "Dragnet" theme with the audience before you begin; they chant it back to you when you say, "Theme music, please."

As the scene opens...

Joe Friday and phone are stage right, Lot and his two daughters are stage left (or vice versa).

Theme music, please. It was a Friday afternoon in Homicide, and the suave and streetwise police sergeant Joe Friday was practicing his kung fu moves. He started with a leg kick. Then he did a karate chop. Next came a behind-the-back punch. Then a flying ballerina kick. Finally he did a classic kung fu fall.

The phone rang. Friday picked up the receiver and listened. His face expressed horror. Then concentration. Then curiosity. Then he spoke: "Ten-four. I'll be right over."

With siren blaring, Friday raced to the site of what appeared to have been a devastating fire. He explored the crime scene and made notes. Unfortunately, he forgot that the site was still hot, and his feet got very hot. Friday jumped around and complained about his hot feet.

Theme music, please.

It was only a matter of moments before he bumped into a man named Lot, who stood in the middle of the smoldering ruins, weeping and beating his chest. Friday immediately frisked Lot and asked him what was going on. Lot continued weeping uncontrollably. He said, "My wife, she's been a-salted." Friday looked down and, sure enough—there was a small mound of salt. He picked up a pinch and threw it over his shoulder for good luck. Unfortunately, the salt went in Lot's eyes, which only intensified his uncontrollable weeping.

Surveying the scene, Friday spoke to Lot's two daughters, who recounted the awful story of the a-salt.

Theme music, please. *(clear the stage)*

It had been a typical day in Gomorrah. The people were drunk, shooting up drugs, fighting, and listening to Jimmy Buffet CDs. Lot was sitting in the gate of the city when he was approached by two angels, who flapped their wings and danced around Lot, like ballerinas. It was really quite stunning.

Lot motioned for them to come to his house for the evening. While Lot and his family were dining with them—laughing, playing cards, and enjoying their favorite dessert, angel food cake—an unruly mob surrounded the house, yelling, and pounding on the door, screaming for Lot to let the angels come outside so they could rough them up.

Theme music, please.

The angels got angry and began to flap their wings wildly. Together they told Lot: "Get your family out of here. God is gonna judge this city and its people—we're talking cosmic barbecue. And don't look back, or you'll turn to salt."

Theme music, please.

Lot grabbed his wife and daughters and, in what looked like slow motion, began to run from the town. They ran hand in hand in slow-mo, their faces contorted with desperate fear.

And that's when it happened.

Lot's wife turned, looked back—and immediately began to sink to the ground into a pile of salt. Lot reached for her and tried to shake her. But doing this, Lot the salt shaker continued to keep his eyes turned away from the destruction of Sodom. Gradually being reduced to a handful of sodium, Lot's wife swirled around, coughing, crying, and moaning, "I'm melting...Ah'll be bahck...it's a wonderful life...may the force be with you," and other exit lines from her favorite movies. She had watched lots of cable during her years in Sodom.

Theme music, please.

Friday shook his head. Lot was still weeping uncontrollably, wiping salt out of his eyes. His daughters tried to comfort him by hugging him, patting his hand, and saying encouraging things like, "Dad, just think how much money we'll save on salt!"

Friday took a long puff on his pipe. He coughed from the long puff. It was a clear case of disobedience to God's instructions. Nothing more he could do here—for it was a clear case of a salt with a deadly woman.

Theme music please. ✽

Josephine's Dreams

Bible text

¹Jacob lived in the land where his father had stayed, the land of Canaan.

²This is the account of Jacob.

Joseph, a young man of seventeen, was tending the flocks with his brothers, the sons of Bilhah and the sons of Zilpah, his father's wives, and he brought their father a bad report about them.

³Now Israel loved Joseph more than any of his other sons, because he had been born to him in his old age; and he made a richly ornamented robe for him. ⁴When his brothers saw that their father loved him more than any of them, they hated him and could not speak a kind word to him.

⁵Joseph had a dream, and when he told it to his brothers, they hated him all the more. ⁶He said to them, "Listen to this dream I had: ⁷We were binding sheaves of grain out in the field when suddenly my sheaf rose and stood upright, while your sheaves gathered around mine and bowed down to it."

⁸His brothers said to him, "Do you intend to reign over us? Will you actually rule us?" And they hated him all the more because of his dream and what he had said.

⁹Then he had another dream, and he told it to his brothers. "Listen," he said, "I had another dream, and this time the sun and moon and eleven stars were bowing down to me."

¹⁰When he told his father as well as his brothers, his father rebuked him and said, "What is this dream you had? Will your mother and I and your brothers actually come and bow down to the ground before you?" ¹¹His brothers were jealous of him, but his father kept the matter in mind.

¹²Now his brothers had gone to graze their father's flocks near Shechem, ¹³and Israel said to Joseph, "As you know, your brothers are grazing the flocks near Shechem. Come, I am going to send you to them."

"Very well," he replied.

¹⁴So he said to him, "Go and see if all is well with your brothers and with the flocks, and bring word back to me." Then he sent him off from the Valley of Hebron.

When Joseph arrived at Shechem, ¹⁵a man found him wandering around in the fields and asked him, "What are you looking for?"

¹⁶He replied, "I'm looking for my brothers. Can you tell me where they are grazing their flocks?"

¹⁷"They have moved on from here," the man answered. "I heard them say, 'Let's go to Dothan.'"

So Joseph went after his brothers and found them near Dothan. ¹⁸But they saw him in the distance, and before he reached them, they plotted to kill him.

¹⁹"Here comes that dreamer!" they said to each other. ²⁰"Come now, let's kill him and throw him into one of these cisterns and say that a ferocious animal devoured him. Then we'll see what comes of his dreams."

²¹When Reuben heard this, he tried to rescue him from their hands. "Let's not take his life," he said. ²²"Don't shed any blood. Throw him into this cistern here in the desert, but don't lay a hand on him." Reuben said this to rescue him from them and take him back to his father.

²³So when Joseph came to his brothers, they stripped him of his robe—the richly ornamented robe he was wearing—

²⁴and they took him and threw him into the cistern. Now the cistern was empty; there was no water in it.

²⁵As they sat down to eat their meal, they looked up and saw a caravan of Ishmaelites coming from Gilead. Their camels were loaded with spices, balm and myrrh, and they were on their way to take them down to Egypt.

²⁶Judah said to his brothers, "What will we gain if we kill our brother and cover up his blood? ²⁷Come, let's sell him to the Ishmaelites and not lay our hands on him; after all, he is our brother, our own flesh and blood." His brothers agreed.

²⁸So when the Midianite merchants came by, his brothers pulled Joseph up out of the cistern and sold him for twenty shekels of silver to the Ishmaelites, who took him to Egypt.

Cast

* Josephine (small female)
* Jacob
* Josephine's brothers and sisters (3-10 people)
* Josephine's bed (male)
* Ish Malite (big male, strong enough to carry Josephine)
* The youth group (everyone else)

Props

* '70s clothes (optional)
* Strobe light (could be improvised)
* Tree branches
* "Sticky stars" (self-adhesive star-shaped stickers)
* Moon Pie
* Rope and gag (could be a handkerchief or bandanna)
* Gunny sack (big enough to fit Josephine)

Leader hints

A strobe light adds a nice effect to the dream sequence, if you can get or improvise one. When Josephine is dreaming, the brothers and sisters (and Jacob) act out the dream. And it's good if Josephine knows the hand motions to the song "Pharaoh, Pharaoh," or at least can improvise them. Finally, when the brothers and sisters make their final entrance (into the youth group), they enter from the back of the room.

As the scene opens...

Josephine's room is a corner of the stage; the "bed" is lying on the ground, or on some chairs. Josephine and her brothers and sisters are center stage. Jacob enters stage left, strobe light in hand. Ish Malite enters stage right. For the last half of the melodrama, Josephine's house becomes instead the youth room. The audience will be the youth group.

On Josephine's seventeenth birthday her dad, Jacob, threw her a '70s party—during which he presented her with a beautiful strobe light. When Josephine's brothers and sisters saw this, they became very jealous, because they had gotten only flashlights for their birthdays. Josephine held up the strobe and danced around the room, showing it to each of her brothers and sisters. All she got in return, however, were fake smiles—and then her siblings huddled together, whispering and pointing at her as they talked. Josephine was sad and lonely—but she was still very excited about her strobe light, so she took it into her room, plugged it in, and got in bed to watch it. But she soon fell into a deep sleep and dreamed this dream.

Josephine dreamed that her brothers and sisters carried tree branches into her room, fell to their knees, bowed before her, and then left her room. Josephine snored, and turned over on her bed. Then she dreamed a second dream: her brothers and sisters came in with stars on their foreheads, and her dad came in with a Moon Pie. They all fell to their knees again and bowed before her. Then she dreamed that they all left again.

You know, it was amazing how real her dreams seemed.

She awoke, rolled over on her bed, unplugged her strobe light, and went outside, calling all her brothers and sisters around her. Speechless because of the shocking nature of her dreams, she could describe her dreams only by using her hands. They all rolled their eyes, folded their arms, and walked away.

Josephine sadly returned to her room and sat down on her bed. At that moment, Josephine's brothers and sisters stormed into her room, put a gag in her mouth, tied a rope around her, shoved her under her bed, and left the room. The bed yelled in pain.

About that time, along came a man from the Salvation Army to see if the family had anything to give away. The man's name was Ish Malite. When he knocked on the door, Jacob let him in—and then left the room so he could finish watching Ricki Lake *(or your TV talk show of choice)*, whose show that day was about sibling rivalry in dysfunctional families. With Jacob out of the room, and Ish Malite's back turned, Josephine's brothers and sisters pulled her out from under her bed, stashed her in a gunny sack, and gave her to Mr. Malite.

"Here's some old stuff you can have," they told him.

"Why, thank you very much," he said. He waved goodbye to them, and went on his way.

Mr. Malite's next stop was at a church to see if they had anything to give away. He walked in and saw a youth group sitting there. At that moment they all stood and sang at the top of their lungs:

Pharaoh, Pharaoh, oh baby, let my people go!

Mr. Malite was so surprised he dropped his bag. He was even more surprised when Josephine yelped, then crawled out of the bag. He'd heard of letting the cat out of the bag, but this was ridiculous. He took one look at her, and fainted. Someone from the youth group untied Josephine and removed her gag. Now "Pharaoh, Pharaoh" was Josephine's favorite song, and she told the youth group she knew the hand motions. She demonstrated them while singing the chorus, after which the youth group stood up and imitated her every move. After singing the chorus together, the youth group was so excited they began bowing to Josephine and chanting, "We are not worthy, we are not worthy, we are not worthy." This went on for some time.

Meanwhile, Josephine's brothers and sisters felt guilty for what they'd done, so they followed Mr. Malite. When they came to the church, they came into the youth room by the back door, and worked their way into the middle of the youth group. They couldn't see Josephine, but they <u>did</u> see the youth group bowing—so they started bowing, too. Then they saw Josephine—and realized that they were bowing to her. So Josephine's dream had come true after all.

A few big guys from the youth group lifted Josephine up onto their shoulders. The youth group cheered. They wanted her to become their president. Josephine's brothers and sisters tried to sneak out the back of the room by crawling under chairs—but Josephine spotted them and called them to the front of the room. The youth group stared at them in silence. Even Mr. Malite sat up—but he was in such shock over what was happening, he fainted again.

Everyone wondered what Josephine would do.

She turned to the youth group and said, "I can't join this group unless my brothers and sisters come with me." By this time Mr. Malite had come to his senses again and was standing—but when he heard what Josephine said, he fainted again. The brothers and sisters gathered around Josephine and gave her a group hug. Then the youth group broke out in one final chorus of "Pharaoh, Pharaoh." And they all lived happily ever after—especially after they learned a few new songs. ✸

The twelve spies, Numbers 13-14

Bible text

13:1The Lord said to Moses, 2"Send some men to explore the land of Canaan, which I am giving to the Israelites. From each ancestral tribe send one of its leaders."

3So at the Lord's command Moses sent them out from the Desert of Paran. All of them were leaders of the Israelites. 4These are their names:

from the tribe of Reuben, Shammua son of Zaccur;

5from the tribe of Simeon, Shaphat son of Hori;

6from the tribe of Judah, Caleb son of Jephunneh;

7from the tribe of Issachar, Igal son of Joseph;

8from the tribe of Ephraim, Hoshea son of Nun;

9from the tribe of Benjamin, Palti son of Raphu;

10from the tribe of Zebulun, Gaddiel son of Sodi;

11from the tribe of Manasseh (a tribe of Joseph), Gaddi son of Susi;

12from the tribe of Dan, Ammiel son of Gemalli;

13from the tribe of Asher, Sethur son of Michael;

14from the tribe of Naphtali, Nahbi son of Vophsi;

15from the tribe of Gad, Geuel son of Maki.

16These are the names of the men Moses sent to explore the land. (Moses gave Hoshea son of Nun the name Joshua.)

17When Moses sent them to explore Canaan, he said, "Go up through the Negev and on into the hill country. 18See what the land is like and whether the people who live there are strong or weak, few or many. 19What kind of land do they live in? Is it good or bad? What kind of towns do they live in? Are they unwalled or fortified? 20How is the soil? Is it fertile or poor? Are there trees on it or not? Do your best to bring back some of the fruit of the land." (It was the season for the first ripe grapes.)

21So they went up and explored the land from the Desert of Zin as far as Rehob, toward Lebo Hamath. 22They went up through the Negev and came to Hebron, where Ahiman, Sheshai and Talmai, the descendants of Anak, lived. (Hebron had been built seven years before Zoan in Egypt.) 23When they reached the Valley of Eshcol, they cut off a branch bearing a single cluster of grapes. Two of them carried it on a pole between them, along with some pomegranates and figs. 24That place was called the Valley of Eshcol because of the cluster of grapes the Israelites cut off there. 25At the end of forty days they returned from exploring the land.

26They came back to Moses and Aaron and the whole Israelite community at Kadesh in the Desert of Paran. There they reported to them and to the whole assembly and showed them the fruit of the land. 27They gave Moses this account: "We went into the land to which you sent us, and it does flow with milk and honey! Here is its fruit. 28But the people who live there are powerful, and the cities are fortified and very large. We even saw descendants of Anak there. 29The Amalekites live in the Negev; the Hittites, Jebusites and Amorites live in the hill country; and the Canaanites live near the sea and along the Jordan."

30Then Caleb silenced the people before Moses and said, "We should go up and take possession of the land, for we can certainly do it."

31But the men who had gone up with him said, "We can't attack those people; they are stronger than we are." 32And they spread among the Israelites a bad report about the land they had explored. They said, "The land we explored devours those living in it. All the people we saw there are of great size. 33We saw the Nephilim there (the descendants of Anak come from the Nephilim). We seemed like grasshoppers in our own eyes, and we looked the same to them."

14:1That night all the people of the community raised their voices and wept aloud. 2All the Israelites grumbled against Moses and Aaron, and the whole assembly said to them, "If only we had died in Egypt! Or in this desert! 3Why is the Lord bringing us to this land only to let us fall by the sword? Our wives and children will be taken as plunder. Wouldn't it be better for us to go back to Egypt?" 4And they said to each other, "We should choose a leader and go back to Egypt."

5Then Moses and Aaron fell facedown in front of the whole Israelite assembly gathered there. 6Joshua son of Nun and Caleb son of Jephunneh, who were among those who had explored the land, tore their clothes 7and said to the entire Israelite assembly, "The land we passed through and explored is exceedingly good. 8If the Lord is pleased with us, he will lead us into that land, a land flowing with milk and honey, and will give it to us. 9Only do not rebel against the Lord. And do not be afraid of the people of the land, because we will swallow them up. Their protection is gone, but the Lord is with us. Do not be afraid of them."

Cast

* Josh (male)
* Kay (female)
* Spies (3-10 people)
* Moe (male)
* Grocer (female)
* Neighbors (the audience)
* Emil Kites (the tallest person in the audience)
* Jeb Usite (the person seated in the farthest corner of the audience)

Props

* Notepads and pencils (for Josh, Kay, and the other spies)
* T-shirts that can be ripped (2)
* Picture or snapshot of some scenery (for Moe)
* Empty milk cartons (5-10)
* Honey jars (for the grocer; 3-8)
* Table
* Chairs (2)

Leader hints

Josh and Kay wear their T-shirts over their clothes.

As the scene opens...

Josh, Kay, and the spies are onstage with their notepads and pencils. Moe and the grocer are both offstage; they'll enter when introduced. Emil Kites and Jeb Usite are seated in the audience. One side of the stage is designated as the grocery store, where there's a table; the milk and honey sit there.

Once there was a group of friends who would get together every weekend to play I Spy. Each weekend they'd meet in a different location, for the object of the game was to search all around and record on their notepads as many objects as they could find. They looked high and low, they stood on their tiptoes, they and crawled around on the ground. They would even bend down and look between their legs, just to get a different perspective.

The two who were best at the game were Josh (the adopted son of a nun) and Kay Lub. They always found the most things, so the others eventually stopped looking, gathered into a big huddle, and peered at them jealously. But Josh and Kay were too busy inspecting the area and taking notes to notice.

One day a man named Moe heard about the spies, so he came and knocked on their door with an assignment. When they opened the door, all the spies began searching him, taking furious notes about every detail. He realized he had come to the right place. He showed them a picture of some cane fields he inherited and said, "I want you to search out this cane land and find out if it's good for me to settle in." He wanted to know what kind of neighbors he would have, and whether or not there was any milk or honey available at the stores. The spies looked at each other and shrugged. They thought it sounded a little funny, but they took notes and said in unison, "We'll get right on it!"

They arrived at the cane land and immediately went to the local store, whose grocer directed them to gallons of milk and shelves of honey. They were so excited they all gave her a hug. Then they went to check on the neighbors. The spies walked through the audience, taking notes on every detail. They made some of the audience members stand up so they could measure how tall they were. The spies made faces at others to try to make them laugh so they could determine how friendly they were.

Finally they all met together at the front of the room. Moe came in and all the spies—except Josh and Kay—ran up to him with their notepads, shouting fearfully, "Milk and honey and neighbors—oh, my!" (chanted as the "lions and tigers and bears—oh my!" line from "The Wizard of Oz") Chaos broke loose as they began skipping around the room, repeating this phrase over and over. Finally Josh and Kay stood up on some chairs and screamed, "SILENCE!" And everyone stopped talking.

Kay said to Moe, "The cane land is good and ripe for settling." But the others rebelled against Kay, pointing to the neighbors in the audience and shaking with fear. They were especially afraid of the tallest one named Emil Kites, and the one way out in the country named Jeb Usite. When the two of them stood up, all the spies—except Josh and Kay—got on the ground and began to hop around the room like grasshoppers.

Josh was so disgusted he tore his shirt. Then Kay tore hers. Everyone covered their eyes until they realized that Kay had another shirt on underneath. Moe fell face down before the spies and said,

"What should I do?"

Josh and Kay said together, "Go!"

The other spies said together, "No!"

The audience said, "Moe!"

Moe looked up and said, "Yeah?"

And everyone sang the Mr. Rogers's song in unison, "Won't you please, won't you please, please won't you be our neighbor?"

Moe was touched by the song, even though it was a little off key. But he waited forty years to make a decision because of the spies' report. He never did live in the cane lands, for he died before moving day. But he left his land to Josh and Kay, who eventually bought new shirts and opened a detective agency. ✷

The battle of Jericho, Joshua 6

Soul Train 'Round the City

Bible text

[1]Now Jericho was tightly shut up because of the Israelites. No one went out and no one came in.

[2]Then the Lord said to Joshua, "See, I have delivered Jericho into your hands, along with its king and its fighting men. [3]March around the city once with all the armed men. Do this for six days. [4]Have seven priests carry trumpets of rams' horns in front of the ark. On the seventh day, march around the city seven times, with the priests blowing the trumpets. [5]When you hear them sound a long blast on the trumpets, have all the people give a loud shout; then the wall of the city will collapse and the people will go up, every man straight in."

[6]So Joshua son of Nun called the priests and said to them, "Take up the ark of the covenant of the Lord and have seven priests carry trumpets in front of it." [7]And he ordered the people, "Advance! March around the city, with the armed guard going ahead of the ark of the Lord."

[8]When Joshua had spoken to the people, the seven priests carrying the seven trumpets before the Lord went forward, blowing their trumpets, and the ark of the Lord's covenant followed them. [9]The armed guard marched ahead of the priests who blew the trumpets, and the rear guard followed the ark. All this time the trumpets were sounding. [10]But Joshua had commanded the people, "Do not give a war cry, do not raise your voices, do not say a word until the day I tell you to shout. Then shout!" [11]So he had the ark of the Lord carried around the city, circling it once. Then the people returned to camp and spent the night there.

[12]Joshua got up early the next morning and the priests took up the ark of the Lord. [13]The seven priests carrying the seven trumpets went forward, marching before the ark of the Lord and blowing the trumpets. The armed men went ahead of them and the rear guard followed the ark of the Lord, while the trumpets kept sounding. [14]So on the second day they marched around the city once and returned to the camp. They did this for six days.

[15]On the seventh day, they got up at daybreak and marched around the city seven times in the same manner, except that on that day they circled the city seven times. [16]The seventh time around, when the priests sounded the trumpet blast, Joshua commanded the people, "Shout! For the Lord has given you the city! [17]The city and all that is in it are to be devoted to the Lord. Only Rahab the prostitute and all who are with her in her house shall be spared, because she hid the spies we sent. [18]But keep away from the devoted things, so that you will not bring about your own destruction by taking any of them. Otherwise you will make the camp of Israel liable to destruction and bring trouble on it. [19]All the silver and gold and the articles of bronze and iron are sacred to the Lord and must go into his treasury."

[20]When the trumpets sounded, the people shouted, and at the sound of the trumpet, when the people gave a loud shout, the wall collapsed; so every man charged straight in, and they took the city. [21]They devoted the city to the Lord and destroyed with the sword every living thing in it — men and women, young and old, cattle, sheep and donkeys.

[22]Joshua said to the two men who had spied out the land, "Go into the prostitute's house and bring her out and all who belong to her, in accordance with your oath to her." [23]So the young men who had done the spying went in and brought out Rahab, her father and mother and brothers and all who belonged to her. They brought out her entire family and put them in a place outside the camp of Israel.

²⁴Then they burned the whole city and everything in it, but they put the silver and gold and the articles of bronze and iron into the treasury of the Lord's house. ²⁵But Joshua spared Rahab the prostitute, with her family and all who belonged to her, because she hid the men Joshua had sent as spies to Jericho — and she lives among the Israelites to this day.

Cast

* Joshua
* Armed men (2)
* Rahab
* Priests (2)
* Walls (4)

Props

* Red licorice rope (a long one)
* Mustard (regular, in squeeze bottle)
* Mustard (Grey Poupon, in jar)

Leader hints

This script works best with an animated Rahab and Joshua. Get the priests to pantomime playing trumpets. The mustard moments in the script are puns on "mustered," as in "Joshua mustered his troops."

As the scene opens...

The four people playing the walls are onstage, standing in a square, shoulder to shoulder, facing outward. The rest of the cast is offstage and enter from the left. When Rahab enters, she has the licorice rope looped around her neck like a scarf.

Jericho was a well-fortified city, enclosed by four impressive walls. I mean, look at those impressive walls! The walls fit together very snugly and were tightly shut up. They were strong and mighty and intended to protect the inhabitants. The walls intimidated outsiders who approached them. "Shut up!" the walls would shout to strangers. Yet if you listened closely, you could hear the walls creak and cramp.

The only person brave enough to come out of hiding was Rahab, the town flirt who climbed up and sat on top of the walls. She tossed her hair like she did whenever she wanted attention. This time, however, she wasn't merely flirting—she had some espionage to do. She took a long red rope from around her neck and tied it around the head of the most impressive wall *(or the wall facing the audience)*.

The rope was a signal to the invading army that she alone was to be spared the impending destruction.

Meanwhile, Joshua—the hip deejay and general of the Israelite army—stood at a distance pondering the impregnable city before him. How could he possibly conquer such a sturdy structure? Suddenly, in a moment of rapturous enlightenment, Joshua got an idea—and the idea made him dance and leap about for joy.

Grabbing his squeeze bottle, he mustered his troops by squirting the mustard right in their noses. They quickly snapped to attention. Like the old war dog he was, Joshua howled in their faces and cried, "Have I got an idea for you! Somebody stop me—I'm ssssssssmokin'! *(in the style of Jim Carrey in "The Mask")*.

The plan was simple. Joshua lined up his forces for a spiritual parade—a kind of Soul Train that would topple the walls of Jericho. The armed men lined up first. They took their shirts off and flexed their massive biceps to intimidate the opposition. Next came the two priests, each carrying his own trumpet. Joshua then took the lead. Upon his command—a long, loud, groovin' 1970s cry of "Soul Train!"—the parade moved out.

Once a day for six days they marched around the city. As they marched the audience counted their laps in Spanish. At the end of the march, the priests lifted their trumpets, licked their lips, and blew those trumpets. The trumpets produced a hideous, blood-curdling blast akin to a scream. There was one blow and one blast for each of the six laps around Jericho.

Meanwhile, all this noise made Rahab hungry. She began eating the red rope tied around the wall. Too bland, she thought. So she yelled down to Joshua to pass the Grey Poupon, which she applied liberally to the rope as she continued to eat it.

The final march was the biggest of all. On the seventh day Joshua reassembled his troops in original parade order, although this time the priests stuck their trumpets in their back pockets. He gave his "Soul Train!" cry again, and the entire group formed a conga line and began dancing around the walls of Jericho seven times, as Joshua sang, "Come on, baby, let's do the conga."

It was more than the walls could handle. Their shoulders heaved as they began giggling, guffawing, and finally belly-laughing hilariously at poor Joshua and this ridiculous Jewish-Cuban dance. But as the walls shook, their foundations were loosened—and the walls collapsed inward with a mighty crash. Rahab, though, fell into Joshua's arms, squealing like a schoolgirl. Awestruck, the two surveyed the utter destruction. Then they joined the others as the entire procession did the conga offstage and into the sunset. ❊

Samson and Delilah, Judges 16

The Young and the Hairless

Bible text

¹One day Samson went to Gaza, where he saw a prostitute. He went in to spend the night with her. ²The people of Gaza were told, "Samson is here!" So they surrounded the place and lay in wait for him all night at the city gate. They made no move during the night, saying, "At dawn we'll kill him."

³But Samson lay there only until the middle of the night. Then he got up and took hold of the doors of the city gate, together with the two posts, and tore them loose, bar and all. He lifted them to his shoulders and carried them to the top of the hill that faces Hebron.

⁴Some time later, he fell in love with a woman in the Valley of Sorek whose name was Delilah. ⁵The rulers of the Philistines went to her and said, "See if you can lure him into showing you the secret of his great strength and how we can overpower him so we may tie him up and subdue him. Each one of us will give you eleven hundred shekels of silver."

⁶So Delilah said to Samson, "Tell me the secret of your great strength and how you can be tied up and subdued."

⁷Samson answered her, "If anyone ties me with seven fresh thongs that have not been dried, I'll become as weak as any other man."

⁸Then the rulers of the Philistines brought her seven fresh thongs that had not been dried, and she tied him with them. ⁹With men hidden in the room, she called to him, "Samson, the Philistines are upon you!" But he snapped the thongs as easily as a piece of string snaps when it comes close to a flame. So the secret of his strength was not discovered.

¹⁰Then Delilah said to Samson, "You have made a fool of me; you lied to me. Come now, tell me how you can be tied."

¹¹He said, "If anyone ties me securely with new ropes that have never been used, I'll become as weak as any other man."

¹²So Delilah took new ropes and tied him with them. Then, with men hidden in the room, she called to him, "Samson, the Philistines are upon you!" But he snapped the ropes off his arms as if they were threads.

¹³Delilah then said to Samson, "Until now, you have been making a fool of me and lying to me. Tell me how you can be tied."

He replied, "If you weave the seven braids of my head into the fabric on the loom and tighten it with the pin, I'll become as weak as any other man." So while he was sleeping, Delilah took the seven braids of his head, wove them into the fabric ¹⁴and tightened it with the pin.

Again she called to him, "Samson, the Philistines are upon you!" He awoke from his sleep and pulled up the pin and the loom, with the fabric.

¹⁵Then she said to him, "How can you say, 'I love you,' when you won't confide in me? This is the third time you have made a fool of me and haven't told me the secret of your great strength." ¹⁶With such nagging she prodded him day after day until he was tired to death.

¹⁷So he told her everything. "No razor has ever been used on my head," he said, "because I have been a Nazirite set apart to God since birth. If my head were shaved, my strength would leave me, and I would become as weak as any other man."

¹⁸When Delilah saw that he had told her everything, she sent word to the rulers of the Philistines, "Come back once more; he has told me everything." So the rulers of the Philistines returned with the silver in their hands. ¹⁹Having put him to sleep on her lap, she called a man to shave off the seven braids of his hair,

and so began to subdue him. And his strength left him.

²⁰Then she called, "Samson, the Philistines are upon you!"

He awoke from his sleep and thought, "I'll go out as before and shake myself free." But he did not know that the Lord had left him.

²¹Then the Philistines seized him, gouged out his eyes and took him down to Gaza. Binding him with bronze shackles, they set him to grinding in the prison. ²²But the hair on his head began to grow again after it had been shaved.

Cast

* Handsome
* DeLiar
* Phyllis
* The Phyllis Teens (3-5 females)

Props

* Bungee cord
* Sandals
* Hand mirror
* Blindfold
* Gag
* Rope

As the scene opens...

Handsome is in his house, preparing for his date with DeLiar.

In our last episode of "The Young and the Hairless," we saw the hunky, long-haired, studmuffin Handsome as he got ready to visit that passion princess DeLiar. He held up a mirror, looking at himself, combing the 'do. He flexed his pecs. He smoothed his eyebrows. All the while he was humming: "There he is, Mr. America..."

Unbeknownst to Handsome, at that very moment, in the Valley of Sorek, sweet little ol' DeLiar was hatching a plot with the neighborhood tough girl, Phyllis, and her gang of strong, mean women with an attitude—and with unshaved armpits: the Phyllis Teens. They huddled together and talked in low voices. They chuckled quietly. With her head in the huddle, Phyllis growled, "I want to know the secret of Handsome's strength."

The Phyllis Teens slapped each other on the back, and yelled in unison,

We are woman, hear us roar!
Handsome ain't gonna be strong no more!

Later that night DeLiar was in her apartment, laughing at her favorite TV show, "Bethlehem, 90210." There was a knock at the door—and in strolled Handsome! He swooped her into his arms, and gave her a long, romantic...handshake. He spoke: "Greetings, my little cactus blossom."

DeLiar looked into Handsome's face and gave a sexy wink. Then she gave him a flirty smile and said, "That was some handshake, you hunka hunka burnin' love. By the way, big guy, what's the secret of your strength?" With that, she began to run her hands up and down his arm. Handsome flexed his forearm so she could feel his muscle.

With a wink of his eye and a flashy grin, Handsome replied: "It's my thong sandals, DeLiar. Undo the velcro, and I'm just a scrawny weakling."

So she looked at him with her flirty smile and said, "May I try on your sandals? I have a thing for thongs."

Handsome, thinking himself very funny replied, "Oh great, I love music too. What thong should I thing?"

But DeLiar slid closer to Handsome and put her finger over his mouth in a shut-up gesture. Obviously enchanted by her magic, Handsome began slipping off his sandals.

Just then, the Phyllis Teens ran into the room and attacked Handsome. They swarmed all over him. But Handsome jumped to his feet and did a series of karate moves that left these tough adolescent women falling in every direction. And so his secret remained undis- covered—barely.

But DeLiar was ticked off. She ran to Handsome and slapped him senseless. She whined, "That was rude, Handsome! You lied to me! Now...tell me really the real secret of your strength." And she began walking her fingers up his arm all the way to his ear. Then she stuck one of her fingers in his ear and said, "Can you hear me, big guy?"

Handsome was breathing heavily. He shook his head to clear his thinking, but he was obviously under the spell of DeLiar. He said, "If you tie me with three bungee cords that have never been used, I will not be able to break free."

And with that, DeLiar suggested sweetly, "Well, speaking of bungee cords, let's practice some bungee jumping right here from the living room chandelier! Here, I'll tie your hands."

But no sooner were Handsome's hands tied than the Phyllis Teens stormed into the room again, screaming and hitting Handsome. Yet once again our hero was too clever. Handsome reached up to the chandelier, grabbed the bungee cord, and flailed it wildly at the Phyllis Teens until, one by one, they fell away.

Now DeLiar was really upset. She pouted, "I've tried to have you captured twice, and you haven't been nice to my friends!" DeLiar reached out and took Handsome's hands. She whined, "Doesn't our relationship mean anything? Can't I trust you?"

As she spoke, DeLiar rubbing his arms, felt his muscles, tickled his kneecap, batted her eyes, and scrunched her nose. Then she said, "If you really loved me, you know, you'd give in."

And finally Handsome did give in. In his best playboy voice he said, "The secret of my strength is...my hair."

The audience gasped. They said all together, "Oh darn! Oh fudge! Oh no!"

With that, Handsome laid his head down in DeLiar's lap as DeLiar sang quietly, "Rock a bye, baby..." When Handsome was fast asleep, DeLiar gave him a massive buzz haircut, making razor sounds as she worked.

It wasn't long before the Phyllis Teens charged into the room again, screaming, swinging, and kicking. This time Handsome was no match for the raging women. They blindfolded and gagged him. The audience gasped. They tied his hands. The audience groaned. They took him prisoner and danced around Handsome like Indians doing a war dance.

Unfortunately, that's all the time we have for today's episode of "The Young and the Hairless." Tune in next time when Handsome says, "Lord, remember me, just once more," and when DeLiar says, "Man, those burritos were awesome."

The moral to the story: never trust anyone who pressures you to give in for love, for you may lose much more than your hair. ✻

The disobedience of Saul, 1 Samuel 13

Caveheart

Bible text

¹Saul was thirty years old when he became king, and he reigned over Israel forty-two years.

²Saul chose three thousand men from Israel; two thousand were with him at Micmash and in the hill country of Bethel, and a thousand were with Jonathan at Gibeah in Benjamin. The rest of the men he sent back to their homes.

³Jonathan attacked the Philistine outpost at Geba, and the Philistines heard about it. Then Saul had the trumpet blown throughout the land and said, "Let the Hebrews hear!" ⁴So all Israel heard the news: "Saul has attacked the Philistine outpost, and now Israel has become a stench to the Philistines." And the people were summoned to join Saul at Gilgal.

⁵The Philistines assembled to fight Israel, with three thousand chariots, six thousand charioteers, and soldiers as numerous as the sand on the seashore. They went up and camped at Micmash, east of Beth Aven. ⁶When the men of Israel saw that their situation was critical and that their army was hard pressed, they hid in caves and thickets, among the rocks, and in pits and cisterns. ⁷Some Hebrews even crossed the Jordan to the land of Gad and Gilead.

Saul remained at Gilgal, and all the troops with him were quaking with fear. ⁸He waited seven days, the time set by Samuel; but Samuel did not come to Gilgal, and Saul's men began to scatter. ⁹So he said, "Bring me the burnt offering and the fellowship offerings." And Saul offered up the burnt offering. ¹⁰Just as he finished making the offering, Samuel arrived, and Saul went out to greet him.

¹¹"What have you done?" asked Samuel.

Saul replied, "When I saw that the men were scattering, and that you did not come at the set time, and that the Philistines were assembling at Micmash, ¹²I thought, 'Now the Philistines will come down against me at Gilgal, and I have not sought the Lord's favor.' So I felt compelled to offer the burnt offering."

¹³"You acted foolishly," Samuel said. "You have not kept the command the Lord your God gave you; if you had, he would have established your kingdom over Israel for all time. ¹⁴But now your kingdom will not endure; the Lord has sought out a man after his own heart and appointed him leader of his people, because you have not kept the Lord's command."

Cast

❋ Saul, a.k.a. Caveheart (male)
❋ Samuel (male)
❋ Minstrel (female)
❋ People around the campfire (4)

Props

❋ Spear
❋ Large Bible
❋ Ukelele, banjo, or autoharp
❋ Fake fire in fireplace (optional)

Leader hints

Pacing is important as you read through the melodrama. In fact, read it through by yourself a couple times before you perform it with a group.

Long ago in a far away land where people spoke with very bad Scottish accents, there was a mighty king who ruled over the nation of Israel. His true name was Saul, but storytellers from the old country simply call him Caveheart. He was strong, he was handsome, he was tall in stature, and he spoke with a suspicious Scottish accent. In fact, when he wasn't busy being king, he would practice speaking standard Scottish phrases with an accent—phrases like "Aye, bonnie lassie," and "Aye, 'tis a lovely morning" and "'Tis a cool kilt you're wearing, dude" and "Sorry, captain, but we're out of dilithium crystals."

In many ways, Saul was a great man with many gifts, but he had one very serious problem—well, actually two, counting the accent. He was not willing to fully give himself to God. Sometimes he was very serious about his commitment, praying to God on behalf of his people. Other times he was so divided in his heart that he'd rave inside his house, screaming, rolling around on the floor, counting backwards from ten, and—worst of all—foaming at the mouth.

His servants worried about him so much that they brought in a minstrel to play music and soothe his mind. The minstrel played and sang Saul's favorite Scottish tune:

My bonnie lies over the ocean, my bonnie lies over the sea,
My bonnie lies over the ocean, so bring back my bonnie to me.

Sometimes Caveheart would clap and sing along. Other times he would weep like a baby. Still other times he'd rave with anger. One time he even threw a spear at the minstrel, right in the middle of the song "Pass It On." But the minstrel dodged the spear and just kept singing,

It only takes a spark to get a fire going,
And soon all those around will warm up in its glowing.

Once Caveheart was on the battlefield, encamped with the army of Israel. He majestically looked over the battlefield and furrowed his brow as he thought of his people. His people just happened to be sitting near him, warming their hands around the campfire, singing "Kum Bah Yah" and making funny hand-in-armpit noises. Someone started singing "Pass It On," but King Saul gave him a dirty look and reached for his spear. As he stood there giving dirty looks <u>and</u> majestically looking across the battlefield, he announced the bad news:

"People, we've been surrounded by the army of the Philistines. I fear they will attack. We're history!"

But the people continued to sing "Kum Bah Yah"—in fact, they sang it with even more feeling now: "Someone's history, Lord, kum bah yah..." They used the song's hand motions, and they swayed back and forth as they sang.

Then everything around the campfire was hushed. No swaying, no kum bahing or yahing. For Samuel, the prophet of God, had arrived with a word from the Lord for Saul:

"Saul, you're history. You've been surrounded by the army of the Philistines."

Those around the campfire began humming "Kum Bah Yah" again.

Samuel then gave Saul some very important instructions: "The Lord will give you victory, but you must do as I say. Do not fight the Philistines before I first offer a sacrifice to the Lord."

And with that, Samuel the prophet left the camp.

For seven long days Saul and the army of Israel waited on God, surrounded by the Philistines—who were edging ever closer. By this time the people around the campfire were on verse 35,647 of "Kum Bah Yah," but they were fatigued by now: "Someone's speaking Scottish poorly, Lord, kum bah yah..."

Saul was twiddling his thumbs, rubbing his head, cracking his knuckles, and making popping noises with his finger in his mouth. They waited seven long days, and Samuel still hadn't come back. Singing, twiddling, rubbing, waiting—and still no Samuel.

Finally Caveheart could take it no more. He screamed out with a bad Scottish accent, "We can't wait another day, captain! It won't be long before the whole thing blows! We've got to attack those Klingons—I mean, those Philistines!"

And he quickly ordered the people around the fire to prepare a burnt offering, just as Samuel commanded.

But against Samuel's instructions, Saul offered the sacrifice himself, pronouncing the ritual words:

Red are the roses, wild the gales—
But please keep the Philistines from kicking our tails.

No sooner had he offered the sacrifice than Samuel strode back into camp. Everyone stopped moving. No twiddling, no singing—total quiet as they looked at the anger on Samuel's face. He grabbed Saul by the arms and said, "What have you done here?"

Saul replied, "Your honor, the Philistines had us surrounded. My troops were starting to desert me, you had not come back—and I was sick of that singing!" He started to sob. Through his sobs he said, "So I forced myself to offer the burnt offering."

Samuel looked him straight in the eye and said, "Do you think the Lord wants your phony worship? Do you think he wants you to be religious instead of obedient? Do you really think he even <u>likes</u> "Kum Bah Yah"?

When they heard that, the people around the fire began humming "My Bonnie Lies over the Ocean."

Saul hung his head in shame, for he knew he had been a fool. God would have protected Israel, but Saul had grown impatient. Instead of keeping his eyes on the promise of God, Saul watched the Philistines surround him. Instead of obeying God, King Caveheart caved in to the crowd. ✳

if the Shoe Fits, Crown Him

Bible text

¹The Lord said to Samuel, "How long will you mourn for Saul, since I have rejected him as king over Israel? Fill your horn with oil and be on your way; I am sending you to Jesse of Bethlehem. I have chosen one of his sons to be king."

²But Samuel said, "How can I go? Saul will hear about it and kill me."

The Lord said, "Take a heifer with you and say, 'I have come to sacrifice to the Lord.' ³Invite Jesse to the sacrifice, and I will show you what to do. You are to anoint for me the one I indicate."

⁴Samuel did what the Lord said. When he arrived at Bethlehem, the elders of the town trembled when they met him. They asked, "Do you come in peace?"

⁵Samuel replied, "Yes, in peace; I have come to sacrifice to the Lord. Consecrate yourselves and come to the sacrifice with me." Then he consecrated Jesse and his sons and invited them to the sacrifice.

⁶When they arrived, Samuel saw Eliab and thought, "Surely the Lord's anointed stands here before the Lord."

⁷But the Lord said to Samuel, "Do not consider his appearance or his height, for I have rejected him. The Lord does not look at the things man looks at. Man looks at the outward appearance, but the Lord looks at the heart."

⁸Then Jesse called Abinadab and had him pass in front of Samuel. But Samuel said, "The Lord has not chosen this one either." ⁹Jesse then had Shammah pass by, but Samuel said, "Nor has the Lord chosen this one." ¹⁰Jesse had seven of his sons pass before Samuel, but Samuel said to him, "The Lord has not chosen these." ¹¹So he asked Jesse, "Are these all the sons you have?"

"There is still the youngest," Jesse answered, "but he is tending the sheep."

Samuel said, "Send for him; we will not sit down until he arrives."

¹²So he sent and had him brought in. He was ruddy, with a fine appearance and handsome features.

Then the Lord said, "Rise and anoint him; he is the one."

¹³So Samuel took the horn of oil and anointed him in the presence of his brothers, and from that day on the Spirit of the Lord came upon David in power. Samuel then went to Ramah.

Cast

❋ Sam (male)
❋ Rock (female)
❋ Voice of God (deep-voiced male, or use a microphone)
❋ Jesse (male)
❋ 7 brothers (or 7 siblings)
❋ David (male)
❋ The audience

Props

❋ Rock
❋ Shoe
❋ Cup of water
❋ Doorway (improvise one if necessary, stage left or right)

Leader hints

A cup of water gets thrown on David in this melodrama, so be prepared for a little water on the floor.

As the scene opens...

Jesse and his sons are behind the door, stage left. The rock is onstage; Sam is next to it. The Voice of God is offstage and says all his lines from there; he or she is also holding David's shoe, ready to fling it onstage at the appropriate time. When David walks onstage toward the end of the scene, he wears only one shoe, of course.

One day a prophet named Sam sat on a rock, a very sad expression on his face. He was so sad, in fact, that he began crying softly. His crying became louder. Soon he was sobbing uncontrollably, falling off the rock and beating the ground as he wept.

The rock said in a loud voice, "What's wrong Sam?"

And Sam replied, "I'm crying about Saul, the no-good king." And when he realized he was talking to a rock, he cried even louder.

Suddenly a loud voice bellowed, "Sam, stop crying!"

Sam was stunned. He recognized it as the Voice of God. So he stopped crying and looked around. The Voice said, "Don't mourn for Saul. I've chosen a new king."

And Sam said, "Who, Lord?"

The Voice said, "I'll show you." Then in a western accent the Voice said, "Now get on over to Jesse's place, pardner!"

Sam had never heard God speak that way, so he began to chuckle. His chuckles turned into laughter. Then the rock began laughing. Then the audience began laughing.

And God said, "You laughin' at me?"

Everyone stopped laughing instantly and shook their heads.

Suddenly, out of nowhere, a shoe plopped down next to Sam. And God said, "The person who fits this shoe will be the next king." Sam picked the shoe up and scratched his head. Something about this scenario seemed familiar to him...he looked around to see if there were any pumpkin carriages. Then he dropped the shoe on the rock to see if it was made of glass. The rock cried out in pain. Sam apologized to the rock as he picked up the shoe.

Well, at least this wasn't a scene from Cinderella, Sam thought, so he went over to Jesse's house and knocked on the door. Jesse answered and immediately fell to the ground before Sam. Jesse's sons all came to the door; when they saw Sam, they fell to the ground too, forming a huge dog pile. Sam thought there had been an earthquake, so he fell to the ground, too.

Finally Jesse lifted up his head and said, "Do you come in peace?"

Sam held up a peace sign and said loudly, "Peace!"

So everyone made a peace sign, got up, and gave each other a group hug. Sam stepped out of the huddle and said, "The next king of Israel will be the one who fits this shoe."

All of Jesse's sons lined up, took off one of their shoes, and held out their feet. Then the smell hit them, and everyone plugged their noses. Even the audience had to plug their noses.

Sam walked slowly down the line of sons, looking at their feet, holding the shoe up next to each foot. But he saw that none of these feet fit the shoe, and he shook his head sadly.

At that moment David walked in. He waved to his dad and said, "Hi, Dad—have you seen my shoe?"

The brothers glared at him. But Sam grinned at him. He ran over to David, hugged him, and kneeled down to place the shoe on his foot. The Voice said, "Rise and anoint him—he's the one!"

The brothers said, "We'll anoint him, Sam." And before Sam could stop them, they took a cup of water and poured it on David's head. Sam kneeled and said enthusiastically, "Hail to our king!" The brothers kneeled and said quite unenthusiastically, "Hail to our king." The audience kneeled and said happily, "Hail to our king!"

David wiped his face, vowing then and there never to go near a bath again. Though he did, once. But that's another story. ✻

David and Goliath, 1 Samuel 17

Dave, the Wave, and the Giant Kahuna

Bible text

¹Now the Philistines gathered their forces for war and assembled at Socoh in Judah. They pitched camp at Ephes Dammim, between Socoh and Azekah. ²Saul and the Israelites assembled and camped in the Valley of Elah and drew up their battle line to meet the Philistines. ³The Philistines occupied one hill and the Israelites another, with the valley between them.

⁴A champion named Goliath, who was from Gath, came out of the Philistine camp. He was over nine feet tall. ⁵He had a bronze helmet on his head and wore a coat of scale armor of bronze weighing five thousand shekels; ⁶on his legs he wore bronze greaves, and a bronze javelin was slung on his back. ⁷His spear shaft was like a weaver's rod, and its iron point weighed six hundred shekels. His shield bearer went ahead of him.

⁸Goliath stood and shouted to the ranks of Israel, "Why do you come out and line up for battle? Am I not a Philistine, and are you not the servants of Saul? Choose a man and have him come down to me. ⁹If he is able to fight and kill me, we will become your subjects; but if I overcome him and kill him, you will become our subjects and serve us." ¹⁰Then the Philistine said, "This day I defy the ranks of Israel! Give me a man and let us fight each other." ¹¹On hearing the Philistine's words, Saul and all the Israelites were dismayed and terrified.

¹²Now David was the son of an Ephrathite named Jesse, who was from Bethlehem in Judah. Jesse had eight sons, and in Saul's time he was old and well advanced in years. ¹³Jesse's three oldest sons had followed Saul to the war: The firstborn was Eliab; the second, Abinadab; and the third, Shammah. ¹⁴David was the youngest. The three oldest followed Saul, ¹⁵but David went back and forth from Saul to tend his father's sheep at Bethlehem.

¹⁶For forty days the Philistine came forward every morning and evening and took his stand.

¹⁷Now Jesse said to his son David, "Take this ephah of roasted grain and these ten loaves of bread for your brothers and hurry to their camp. ¹⁸Take along these ten cheeses to the commander of their unit. See how your brothers are and bring back some assurance from them. ¹⁹They are with Saul and all the men of Israel in the Valley of Elah, fighting against the Philistines."

²⁰Early in the morning David left the flock with a shepherd, loaded up and set out, as Jesse had directed. He reached the camp as the army was going out to its battle positions, shouting the war cry. ²¹Israel and the Philistines were drawing up their lines facing each other. ²²David left his things with the keeper of supplies, ran to the battle lines and greeted his brothers. ²³As he was talking with them, Goliath, the Philistine champion from Gath, stepped out from his lines and shouted his usual defiance, and David heard it. ²⁴When the Israelites saw the man, they all ran from him in great fear.

²⁵Now the Israelites had been saying, "Do you see how this man keeps coming out? He comes out to defy Israel. The king will give great wealth to the man who kills him. He will also give him his daughter in marriage and will exempt his father's family from taxes in Israel."

²⁶David asked the men standing near him, "What will be done for the man who kills this Philistine and removes this disgrace from Israel? Who is this uncircumcised Philistine that he should defy the armies of the living God?"

²⁷They repeated to him what they had been saying and told him, "This is what will be done for the man who kills him."

28When Eliab, David's oldest brother, heard him speaking with the men, he burned with anger at him and asked, "Why have you come down here? And with whom did you leave those few sheep in the desert? I know how conceited you are and how wicked your heart is; you came down only to watch the battle."

29"Now what have I done?" said David. "Can't I even speak?" 30He then turned away to someone else and brought up the same matter, and the men answered him as before. 31What David said was overheard and reported to Saul, and Saul sent for him.

32David said to Saul, "Let no one lose heart on account of this Philistine; your servant will go and fight him."

33Saul replied, "You are not able to go out against this Philistine and fight him; you are only a boy, and he has been a fighting man from his youth."

34But David said to Saul, "Your servant has been keeping his father's sheep. When a lion or a bear came and carried off a sheep from the flock, 35I went after it, struck it and rescued the sheep from its mouth. When it turned on me, I seized it by its hair, struck it and killed it. 36Your servant has killed both the lion and the bear; this uncircumcised Philistine will be like one of them, because he has defied the armies of the living God. 37The Lord who delivered me from the paw of the lion and the paw of the bear will deliver me from the hand of this Philistine."

Saul said to David, "Go, and the Lord be with you."

38Then Saul dressed David in his own tunic. He put a coat of armor on him and a bronze helmet on his head. 39David fastened on his sword over the tunic and tried walking around, because he was not used to them.

"I cannot go in these," he said to Saul, "because I am not used to them." So he took them off. 40Then he took his staff in his hand, chose five smooth stones from the stream, put them in the pouch of his shepherd's bag and, with his sling in his hand, approached the Philistine.

41Meanwhile, the Philistine, with his shield bearer in front of him, kept coming closer to David. 42He looked David over and saw that he was only a boy, ruddy and handsome, and he despised him. 43He said to David, "Am I a dog, that you come at me with sticks?" And the Philistine cursed David by his gods. 44"Come here," he said, "and I'll give your flesh to the birds of the air and the beasts of the field!"

45David said to the Philistine, "You come against me with sword and spear and javelin, but I come against you in the name of the Lord Almighty, the God of the armies of Israel, whom you have defied. 46This day the Lord will hand you over to me, and I'll strike you down and cut off your head. Today I will give the carcasses of the Philistine army to the birds of the air and the beasts of the earth, and the whole world will know that there is a God in Israel.47All those gathered here will know that it is not by sword or spear that the Lord saves; for the battle is the Lord's, and he will give all of you into our hands."

48As the Philistine moved closer to attack him, David ran quickly toward the battle line to meet him. 49Reaching into his bag and taking out a stone, he slung it and struck the Philistine on the forehead. The stone sank into his forehead, and he fell facedown on the ground.

50So David triumphed over the Philistine with a sling and a stone; without a sword in his hand he struck down the Philistine and killed him.

Cast

* Dave
* Surfers (3-10)
* Dave's 3 bros (3 of the surfers)
* Saul
* Goliath, a.k.a. Giant Kahuna (large, tall male)
* Ocean (the audience)

Props

* Surfboards (2, can be improvised)
* Surf wax (or something that looks like it)
* Wet suit

* Swimming trunks (for Dave to wear)
* Suntan lotion with SMOOTHSTONE written on it
* Sunglasses

Leader hints

Get your audience to practice a wave before starting this melodrama.

As the scene opens...

The surfers and Saul are on the beach. The audience is the ocean. Dave and the Giant Kahuna are offstage. The waves are created, stadium-style, by the audience. Reserve a couple of chairs in the audience for surfers to stand on in order to act like they're surfing the wave.

Once upon a time, long ago, there was a hot surfing spot called Elah Beach. It lay between two hills. Surfers from far and wide used to camp there, and they'd greet each other with the "hang loose" sign. If they didn't know the hang loose sign, they'd give each other high fives. Then they'd psyche themselves up for their day by shielding their eyes from the sun and looking out over the ocean. They watched the waves roll, from one side of the ocean to the other....audience, this is your cue.

The leader of this group of surfers was Saul. Since he was originally from France, they called themselves the Band de Saulet. (By the way, this name came from a suntan oil, Ban de Soleil.) Saul would walk among the surfers and speak French to them as they waxed their boards.

One day a Giant Kahuna named Goliath came to Elah Beach. He was a big dude, standing head and shoulders above the rest. As he made his way into the ocean, the group of surfers stared at him with their mouths gaping open. As the waves started rolling (audience, that's you), he got out to the middle of the ocean and stood on his board. He soon ruled the ocean and dominated the waves, telling them which way to wave, how high to wave, and how far to wave. Other surfers paddled out and tried to join him, but he'd just knock them off their boards and push them into the ocean. Then the ocean would carry them back to shore.

Well, you can see that Goliath developed a nasty reputation. Soon all the surfers were on the beach huddled together, afraid to get in.

While he was out among the waves, Goliath made up a chant and yelled it:

I'm the Big G—surf's up, my friends.
But if you come in, your time will end!

Then he'd laugh hysterically. The ocean laughed too, but they were laughing because he was such a lousy poet. The other surfers just stayed on the beach, waxing their boards and trying to ignore him.

Around noon Dave arrived, bringing lunches for the Band de Saulet. Three of the surfers were his bros, and they gave him high fives. Suddenly Goliath yelled out his challenge once more:

I'm the Big G—surf's up, my friends.
But if you come in, your time will end!

Dave said, "Who's that?"

All the surfers huddled around Dave, quietly explaining to him what was going on. They all tried to persuade him to leave, pointing out that the beach was just too dangerous for him. But Dave had other plans. He stood in front of the surfers and shocked everyone by saying, "If no one else is going to surf, I will!"

Dave's bros said, "What about the Big G?"

Dave said, "I've got a bigger G on my side." And the surfers cheered.

So Dave went to Saul to ask permission to surf with the Big G. Saul not only gave him permission, but gave him his personal wet suit to wear for the shred. (Shred is surf talk for big wave.) When Dave put the wet suit on, he realized it was two sizes too big, so he took it off and decided he'd go with just his trunks. All he took with him was his Smoothstone sunscreen lotion and his Ray Bans.

As Dave paddled out, the Big G laughed at him and said, "You're just a scrawny wimp. You'll be history in no time."

Dave said, "This day a bigger G has come to rule the ocean. Hang ten, big guy."

The two of them stood up and were just about to catch a wave when the Big G reached over and tried to swat Dave off his board. But a big wave from the ocean stood up and blocked him. Dave grabbed his bottle of Smoothstone lotion and threw it at the Big G's head. The Giant was knocked unconscious and fell down into the waves, where he was dog piled by the ocean.

Dave surfed into shore, striking several surfing poses on the way in and demonstrating his impressive ability. As he got to shore he said, "This is God's ocean now." The surfers cheered. Then the ocean cheered. Then the ocean did one final wave goodbye.

From that day forward, all the surfers left Saul to follow Dave, and Smoothstone surpassed Ban de Soleil as the number one tanning lotion on the market. And all the surfers surfed happily in God's green room for the rest of their days. (By the way, green room is surf language for perfect wave). ✱

Split Decision

Bible text

[16]Now two prostitutes came to the king and stood before him. [17]One of them said, "My Lord, this woman and I live in the same house. I had a baby while she was there with me. [18]The third day after my child was born, this woman also had a baby. We were alone; there was no one in the house but the two of us.

[19]"During the night this woman's son died because she lay on him. [20]So she got up in the middle of the night and took my son from my side while I your servant was asleep. She put him by her breast and put her dead son by my breast. [21]The next morning, I got up to nurse my son— and he was dead! But when I looked at him closely in the morning light, I saw that it wasn't the son I had borne."

[22]The other woman said, "No! The living one is my son; the dead one is yours."

But the first one insisted, "No! The dead one is yours; the living one is mine." And so they argued before the king.

[23]The king said, "This one says, 'My son is alive and your son is dead,' while that one says, 'No! Your son is dead and mine is alive.'"

[24]Then the king said, "Bring me a sword." So they brought a sword for the king. [25]He then gave an order: "Cut the living child in two and give half to one and half to the other."

[26]The woman whose son was alive was filled with compassion for her son and said to the king, "Please, my lord, give her the living baby! Don't kill him!"

But the other said, "Neither I nor you shall have him. Cut him in two!"

[27]Then the king gave his ruling: "Give the living baby to the first woman. Do not kill him; she is his mother."

[28]When all Israel heard the verdict the king had given, they held the king in awe, because they saw that he had wisdom from God to administer justice.

Cast

* Bubbles
* Trixie
* Richard Barsimmons
* Baby (male)
* Doctors and nurses (4-6)
* Solomon

Props

* Pillows (to simulate pregnancy)
* Tape player and oldies cassette
* Baby bottle
* Doll (baby, as close as possible to life size)
* Spoon and glass dish containing brownish glop (to simulate "liquified sausage, eggs, and oatmeal"— mashed overripe bananas will do the trick)

As the scene opens...

The two extremely pregnant women (using pillows for stuffing) are onstage.

Three thousand years ago in the faraway land of Israel, there lived two enormously pregnant women named Bubbles and Trixie. They were so pregnant, they couldn't even see their feet, let alone lace their Nikes.

Overdue as they were—I mean, we're talking ten months pregnant—drastic measures were called for. So the two women invested their last shekels in a personal labor coach, Richard Barsimmons, to try to get their deliveries underway, and pronto. Each day Richard arrived at the appointed time, and each day he said in his infuriatingly chipper voice, "All right ladies—let's sweat out those babies!"

And cranking up the oldies, he put the women through some aerobic activities.

It wasn't long before all this exercise took effect. Bubbles gasped, screamed with everything she had, ran next door to the family birthing center, and soon a bouncing baby boy leaped into Bubbles's arms *(the "baby" can leap from behind the "delivery" chair that Bubbles is sitting in)*, hugged her, and yelled, "Mommy!" Curling up in her arms, mother and baby became a family. Doctors and nurses hovered around them, humming "Brahms's Lullaby." A nurse said, "Feeding time!" and stuck a bottle in the baby's mouth.

Meanwhile, seeing all of this, Trixie became insanely jealous of Bubbles and her new baby. Trixie screamed at Richard, "Sweat me into labor, Richie!"

So Richard swung into action. First he performed several variations of the Heimlich Maneuver. Then he showed her how to do a break-dance back spin. Finally, crying out, "Clear!" Richard tickled her in the ribs, continuing this procedure while the audience counted to ten.

But nothing worked. Trixie was exhausted but still pregnant—or was she, wondered Richard all of a sudden. Whipping out his stethoscope, Richard listened for the baby's heartbeat—but in vain.

"You're not pregnant—you just put on a little weight!" exclaimed Richard to Trixie. Trixie collapsed in despair, rolling back and forth on the floor and she wailed and sobbed.

Richard said, "See ya around," and made his exit by jumping up and down and executing his best cheerleading maneuver.

Suddenly Trixie bolted to her feet with a grim, determined look on her face. "I'll get a baby one way or another," she vowed. And late that night, Trixie grabbed one of her dolls and crept over to Bubbles's house. She tiptoed, she crawled on all fours, she slithered on her belly—until she was in the room where Bubbles and her baby were asleep. Trixie silently picked up the baby, and put the doll in its place. Then, with the baby in her arms, she stole back to her own house.

In the morning, Bubbles woke up and prepared a breakfast of liquified sausage, eggs, and oatmeal. She was dumbfounded when her baby showed absolutely no interest in the gloppy breakfast. She tried to wake him by squeezing his cheeks, kissing his forehead, and drizzling the lumpy, brown liquid on his lips, all the while cooing, "Wake up, baby, this is good for you." But there was no response. Then she took a close look at the baby. She picked it up. She tossed it high in the air and caught it. She examined it again. She tossed it high in the air—and this time let it drop.

"This isn't my baby!" she wailed. And with that she stomped over to Trixie's house and yelled, "I know you have my baby! Give him back!" And Bubbles yanked the baby by the arm, pulling him out of Trixie's house.

Trixie grabbed his other arm and pulled him back. "Hey sister, whattcha doin' messin' with my baby?" she asked with attitude.

"He's not your baby, he's *my* baby," Bubbles yelled, still pulling on the baby's arm.

"I don't think so," Trixie insisted, while pulling with equal force on the baby's other arm. "If he's in this house, that makes him mine, honey. That's the way things work around here."

By this time the two women were yanking him back and forth like a bucksaw as they both cried out, "He's my baby! He's my baby! He's my baby!"

News of this conflict quickly reached the highest offices of the land, and Solomon, king of Israel, decided to intervene. Strutting into Trixie's house, Solomon sized up the situation. Then he said, "You two ladies seem to have a little problem. So let's just chop this little fella in two so you can each have half."

Solomon pulled his sword from its scabard and grabbed the baby. Bubbles was horrified. Trixie, on the other hand, sidled up to Solomon and cooed, "Oh Solly, that's a wonderful idea! You know, I hear you have 999 women in your harem. Ever thought about making it an even thousand?"

But Bubbles only fell down, grabbed the king's ankles, and kissed his feet, begging him to spare the baby. She said, "Please let him live. Give the baby to Trixie if you must, but don't kill him!"

At that moment, Solomon knew he had solved the case. He cast the bloodthirsty Trixie to the ground and dropped the baby in the arms of its real mother. Mother and baby squealed and embraced, patted each other on the head, and began playing Ring around the Rosie. For they were a happy family once again. ✻

Dances with Lions

Bible text

¹It pleased Darius to appoint 120 satraps to rule throughout the kingdom, ²with three administrators over them, one of whom was Daniel. The satraps were made accountable to them so that the king might not suffer loss. ³Now Daniel so distinguished himself among the administrators and the satraps by his exceptional qualities that the king planned to set him over the whole kingdom. ⁴At this, the administrators and the satraps tried to find grounds for charges against Daniel in his conduct of government affairs, but they were unable to do so. They could find no corruption in him, because he was trustworthy and neither corrupt nor negligent. ⁵Finally these men said, "We will never find any basis for charges against this man Daniel unless it has something to do with the law of his God."

⁶So the administrators and the satraps went as a group to the king and said: "O King Darius, live forever! ⁷The royal administrators, prefects, satraps, advisers and governors have all agreed that the king should issue an edict and enforce the decree that anyone who prays to any god or man during the next thirty days, except to you, O king, shall be thrown into the lions' den. ⁸Now, O king, issue the decree and put it in writing so that it cannot be altered — in accordance with the laws of the Medes and Persians, which cannot be repealed." ⁹So King Darius put the decree in writing.

¹⁰Now when Daniel learned that the decree had been published, he went home to his upstairs room where the windows opened toward Jerusalem. Three times a day he got down on his knees and prayed, giving thanks to his God, just as he had done before. ¹¹Then these men went as a group and found Daniel praying and asking God for help. ¹²So they went to the king and spoke to him about his royal decree: "Did you not publish a decree that during the next thirty days anyone who prays to any god or man except to you, O king, would be thrown into the lions' den?"

The king answered, "The decree stands — in accordance with the laws of the Medes and Persians, which cannot be repealed."

¹³Then they said to the king, "Daniel, who is one of the exiles from Judah, pays no attention to you, O king, or to the decree you put in writing. He still prays three times a day." ¹⁴When the king heard this, he was greatly distressed; he was determined to rescue Daniel and made every effort until sundown to save him.

¹⁵Then the men went as a group to the king and said to him, "Remember, O king, that according to the law of the Medes and Persians no decree or edict that the king issues can be changed."

¹⁶So the king gave the order, and they brought Daniel and threw him into the lions' den. The king said to Daniel, "May your God, whom you serve continually, rescue you!"

¹⁷A stone was brought and placed over the mouth of the den, and the king sealed it with his own signet ring and with the rings of his nobles, so that Daniel's situation might not be changed. ¹⁸Then the king returned to his palace and spent the night without eating and without any entertainment being brought to him. And he could not sleep.

¹⁹At the first light of dawn, the king got up and hurried to the lions' den. ²⁰When he came near the den, he called to Daniel in an anguished voice, "Daniel, servant of the living God, has your God, whom you serve continually, been able to rescue you from the lions?"

²¹Daniel answered, "O king, live forever! ²²My God sent his angel, and he shut the mouths of the

lions. They have not hurt me, because I was found innocent in his sight. Nor have I ever done any wrong before you, O king."

²³The king was overjoyed and gave orders to lift Daniel out of the den. And when Daniel was lifted from the den, no wound was found on him, because he had trusted in his God.

²⁴At the king's command, the men who had falsely accused Daniel were brought in and thrown into the lions' den, along with their wives and children. And before they reached the floor of the den, the lions overpowered them and crushed all their bones.

²⁵Then King Darius wrote to all the peoples, nations and men of every language throughout the land:
"May you prosper greatly!

²⁶"I issue a decree that in every part of my kingdom people must fear and reverence the God of Daniel.

"For he is the living God and he endures forever; his kingdom will not be destroyed, his dominion will never end. ²⁷He rescues and he saves; he performs signs and wonders in the heavens and on the earth. He has rescued Daniel from the power of the lions."

²⁸So Daniel prospered during the reign of Darius and the reign of Cyrus the Persian."

Cast

* Big Chief Darius (male)
* Shamu (male)
* Cutcheese (male)
* Daniel (male)
* Lions (2 people, on hands and knees)
* Royal tepee (2 people leaning together, facing each other, with legs spread and palms touching)
* Daniel's tepee (2 people, as above)
* Den of lions (4 people holding hands in a circle; 2 of the 4 could also be Daniel's tepee)

Props

* None

Leader hints

Divide your stage into two parts: the royal tepee of Big Chief Darius on one side, and on the other Daniel's tepee—and, as the plot develops, the den of lions. Small group or limited space? Then simply write three large signs: DANIEL'S TEPEE, ROYAL TEPEE, and LION'S DEN; as the scene changes, have one person walk across the front of the stage displaying the appropriate sign.

As the scene opens...

The four human characters and the two tepees are onstage.

Many many moons ago Big Chief Darius appointed three warriors to help oversee tribal matters for the entire Persian nation: Cutcheese (whose Indian name means "man who makes disgusting smell"), Shamu (whose Indian name means "man who thinks he is large sea mammal"), and Daniel (who had no Indian name because he was from the tribe of Judah).

Shamu and Cutcheese were jealous of Daniel because the Chief liked Daniel very much. He was respected by all the people, even though his name didn't mean anything cool.

Shamu and Cutcheese began to plot and scheme behind Daniel's back. They wanted to turn Big Chief Darius against Daniel, but they knew it'd be difficult since Daniel was a faithful man. After huddling for a moment, they gave each other a special secret Indian handshake; then they let out a loud war whoop that terrified the other Indians in the camp. And for just a few brief moments they danced a we're-gonna-nail-Daniel dance.

That very night Shamu and Cutcheese went to Big Chief Darius. It was clear from the expression on their faces that they were on the warpath. As they entered the tepee of Big Chief Darius, he was busily weaving baskets and working on other Indian handicrafts. As he worked he whistled the melody to "One little, two little, three little Indians..."

Shamu and Cutcheese fell at the feet of their chief and together shouted, "O Big Chief Darius, may you live forever! We have an idea for you!" You see, they wanted Chief Darius to make a new law that forbade any person from praying to any god or man—except to Big Chief Darius. Furthermore, if a person <u>did</u> pray to any god or man except the Chief within the next thirty days, that person would be thrown into the den of lions.

Big Chief Darius nodded thoughtfully for a moment, scratched the stubble of his beard, nodded some more, scratched some more, nodded some more, and then dozed off. When he awoke a moment later he said, "How."

Shamu and Cutcheese looked at each other, then replied in unison, "We just <u>told</u> you how, kimosabe."

Meanwhile, back in his tepee Daniel was practicing some animal calls to use with his next hunting party. First he did a bird call. Then the call of the buffalo. Then a duck call. Then, just in case the hunting party got lucky, the call of an elephant. And then his favorite: just in case the hunting party got unlucky, the call for help.

At that moment a messenger ran into Daniel's tepee with news of the Chief's edict. Daniel read the new law, and you could see on his face that he was confused—then he was surprised, then angry, then worried.

"What's an edict?" he asked.

The messenger told him, and then Daniel realized that the Chief had outlawed prayer—at least prayer to the one true God. So Daniel decided to do yet another one of his favorite calls: he knelt out in front of the door of his tepee where everyone could see him, and he called on the name of the Lord.

And every day—three times every day—Daniel continued his habit of praying, right out in front of his tepee where all could see him.

It wasn't long before word of Daniel's disobedience reached Chief Darius. The Chief was majorly saddened. In fact, he became delirious with grief, and began to ramble incoherently in his native Indian language. You could tell Chief Darius loved Daniel very much.

But Shamu and Cutcheese reminded him of the law he had made. Both of them grabbed one of Darius' hands and said, "O Chief—may you live forever, and may you not even doze off—don't forget about the law you made. Daniel must go to the den of lions."

The chief frowned a deep frown. He knew that if he backed down now, people would think he had been lyin'.

He didn't want to do it—and he hoped against hope that Daniel's God would save him—but Big Chief Darius had no choice but to throw Daniel into the den of lions. Darius wept bitterly as he pushed Daniel inside the den. Then the Chief dozed off again.

It was a long night for the Chief. He tossed and turned in his royal tepee. He snored loudly, then softly, then whimpered like a baby, then snored again.

In the den of lions, meanwhile, Daniel faced two hungry lions licking their chops and pacing around him. First he used sign language to try to convince them they weren't really hungry—and besides, he wouldn't taste good. Then he tried communicating to the lions in their own language, and roared his friendliness at them. They still paced around him, licking their chops. Daniel asked them, "Have you guys ever heard of the Chronicles of Narnia? It's a real cool story about this very, very kind lion named Aslan..."

But nothing worked. The lions still circled him, and they were drooling by now.

In desperation Daniel tried his bird call, his buffalo call, then his elephant call. The only response he got from the lions were growls and mean looks. So he finally did the only other call he knew: his Lord call. He knelt and asked God to save him.

Big Chief Darius hurried to the den next morning, and he couldn't believe his eyes. The lions were sitting quietly with Daniel, and the three of them were playing Rock, Paper, Scissors! The chief was so overjoyed, he gave Daniel a high five, and he gave both lions a high paw.

And not one wound was found on Daniel, because he had trusted in his God.

Shamu and Cutcheese? For their betrayal Darius threw both of them into the den of lions. Immediately the lions jumped on top of the men and began breaking their bones and growling mean things to them in lion language. Shamu and Cutcheese tried to yell for help. Shamu even began making what sounded like whale sounds, but it wasn't long before the lions' den turned into the lions' rumpus room, and then the lions' kitchen.

Big Chief Darius was so amazed that Daniel's God had kept him safe that he gave Daniel a new Indian name: Dances with Lions. And the Chief issued a decree to the whole Persian nation: "Daniel's God is Lord! Let everyone worship him!" ✻

Joe and the Wannafights

Bible text

¹The word of the Lord came to Jonah son of Amittai: ²"Go to the great city of Nineveh and preach against it, because its wickedness has come up before me."

³But Jonah ran away from the Lord and headed for Tarshish. He went down to Joppa, where he found a ship bound for that port. After paying the fare, he went aboard and sailed for Tarshish to flee from the Lord.

⁴Then the Lord sent a great wind on the sea, and such a violent storm arose that the ship threatened to break up. ⁵All the sailors were afraid and each cried out to his own god. And they threw the cargo into the sea to lighten the ship.

But Jonah had gone below deck, where he lay down and fell into a deep sleep. ⁶The captain went to him and said, "How can you sleep? Get up and call on your god! Maybe he will take notice of us, and we will not perish."

⁷Then the sailors said to each other, "Come, let us cast lots to find out who is responsible for this calamity." They cast lots and the lot fell on Jonah.

⁸So they asked him, "Tell us, who is responsible for making all this trouble for us? What do you do? Where do you come from? What is your country? From what people are you?"

⁹He answered, "I am a Hebrew and I worship the Lord, the God of heaven, who made the sea and the land."

¹⁰This terrified them and they asked, "What have you done?" (They knew he was running away from the Lord, because he had already told them so.)

¹¹The sea was getting rougher and rougher. So they asked him, "What should we do to you to make the sea calm down for us?"

¹²"Pick me up and throw me into the sea," he replied, "and it will become calm. I know that it is my fault that this great storm has come upon you."

¹³Instead, the men did their best to row back to land. But they could not, for the sea grew even wilder than before. ¹⁴Then they cried to the Lord, "O Lord, please do not let us die for taking this man's life. Do not hold us accountable for killing an innocent man, for you, O Lord, have done as you pleased." ¹⁵Then they took Jonah and threw him overboard, and the raging sea grew calm. ¹⁶At this the men greatly feared the Lord, and they offered a sacrifice to the Lord and made vows to him. ¹⁷But the Lord provided a great fish to swallow Jonah, and Jonah was inside the fish three days and three nights.

Cast

* Joe
* Wannafights (first two rows of the audience)
* Tammy Tarshee
* Other students at Bible study (1-3)
* Voice of God (offstage)
* Wind (1)
* Rain (1)
* Thunder (1)
* Whale (1-3)

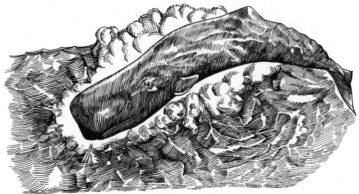

Props

* Bible (for Joe)

Leader hints

If you have the time before the performance of this melodrama, read through the Bible-study scene with Joe and with the Voice of God to get the timing right. While the three of you are doing that, let the people portraying the Whale practice enough to coordinate their actions and work together (one idea: they join hands, and inside the circle of their arms is the whale's stomach).

As the scene opens...

Joe is onstage holding his Bible. The Wannafights are the first two rows of the audience. Tammy and the rest of the Bible study are seated at stage left or right—a far end of the stage, in any case. The rest of the characters are offstage when the skit begins.

One day Joe was on his way to a Bible study at Tammy Tarshee's when he was confronted by a mean and ugly gang known as the Wannafights. Joe knew who they were; their graffiti was all over town. When they saw him, they snarled. Then they growled. Then they shook their fists and began yelling, "Hey you, wanna fight?"

Joe shook his head no. Then the rest of his body began shaking too. They repeated the question over and over. First they said it loudly. Then softly. Then quickly. Then slowly.

Joe did his best to ignore them. He opened his Bible and kept walking toward Tammy's, praying the whole way. When he got there he went inside and joined the Bible study. When it came time for prayer requests, someone suggested they pray for their whale-watching trip, since it could be a good opportunity for outreach. Everyone nodded enthusiastically and agreed, patting each other on the back for being such good Christians.

Then Tammy suggested they pray for the Wannafights. Everyone got really quiet and looked down at the ground. Joe said, "I don't think they deserve prayer." Everyone nodded and agreed. They decided that the Wannafights would have to get a lot nicer before they deserved being prayed for.

They closed their eyes to pray. So did Joe. But suddenly Joe heard the voice of God. It said loudly, "Psssst, hey Joe!"

Joe opened his eyes and said, "Yeah?"

No one else heard the voice of God, so everyone looked at Joe kinda funny. So Joe said, "Uh, yeah, let's pray."

Again they bowed their heads to pray, and once more Joe heard the voice. It said, "Joe!"

This time he looked up, but didn't say anything. Everyone else still had their eyes closed. The voice said, "Joe, this is God. Go tell the Wannafights that I love them."

Joe shook his head no. The voice said, "Joe, I'm not asking you. I'm telling you."

"I can't!" Joe said loudly.

Everyone opened their eyes and stared at Joe. He looked at everyone and said, "I can't, uh, wait for this whale-watching trip!"

Everyone got up, gave each other high fives, then went home.

The time came for the whale-watching trip, and everyone got on the boat. But when the boat got out to sea, a huge storm hit. First the wind came and danced and swirled around the boat. Then the rain and the thunder came and joined the wind, making loud storm noises, spinning around the boat, and doing the tango. The boat, of course, rocked back and forth madly, and all the people went flying from one side of the ship to the other, and back again. And back again. They all got very seasick and began barfing over the side of the ship.

Joe screamed loudly over the wind and rain and the barf, "It's my fault! Throw me in!"

Everyone was so scared, they were willing to try anything. So they picked up Joe and threw him in. Then they threw him a life jacket. Suddenly the storm stopped. The wind and rain and thunder did one final dance step together—and then stood still. Then they rolled offstage. The audience applauded their performance.

The ship headed back to shore, and his friends in his Bible study group waved goodbye to Joe, who was treading water.

"We'll pray for you!" his Bible study group shouted cheerfully.

Then the ship disappeard, and Joe was alone, floating in the water with his life jacket. He started to cry. Then he started to wail. Then he <u>saw</u> a whale. Then he <u>really</u> started to cry. The whale paddled over to him, blubbering and gurgling as it swam. It opened its mouth and swallowed Joe—and then burped very loudly. Joe was so disgusted he fainted. When he came to, he kneeled and began to pray about his attitude. He also prayed for a nicer view. In fact, Joe prayed for three days and three nights—and then the Lord was ready to set him free.

The whale, meanwhile, realized it had eaten something that didn't agree with him. It was a case of in-dye-Joe-stun (*indigestion*). It made the whale groan. The bad pun made the audience groan. The whale rolled around on the sea floor, knocking Joe from one side of its

stomach to the other. Then the whale released some major gas bubbles. Then it got ready to do some major heaving. After two dry
heaves, the whale took a big breath and hurled Joe onto dry land. Joe
knew he was still alive, he wasn't in heaven, because he looked down
at his shirt and saw that he'd been heaved on.

So the Lord told Joe to, first, change shirts, and then to face the
Wannafights. He did both, and soon the Wannafights became know as
the Foundelights. And from that day forward God didn't have to send
Joe by hurling him. Joe just agreed to walk where God wanted him. ✳

Rocky 12: Fight of the Foundations

Bible text

24"Therefore everyone who hears these words of mine and puts them into practice is like a wise man who built his house on the rock. 25The rain came down, the streams rose, and the winds blew and beat against that house; yet it did not fall, because it had its foundation on the rock. 26But everyone who hears these words of mine and does not put them into practice is like a foolish man who built his house on sand. 27The rain came down, the streams rose, and the winds blew and beat against that house, and it fell with a great crash."

Cast

* Sandy Beach (female)
* Rocky (male)
* Tourists (1-3)
* Walls of Rocky's house (2 females)
* Walls of Sandy's house (2 males)
* Stream
* Wind
* Sun

Props

* Boxing clothes for Rocky (optional)

Leader hints

Before the performance of this melodrama, lead the audience in practicing the rainstorm, so they know immediately what to do when the script calls for it. Plus it helps if your youth group is familiar with Amy Grant's song "House of Love"—if they aren't, you may want to drop from the script the three or four allusions to that song.

As the scene opens...

The stage is empty except for Sandy, who lies on the floor on her side, facing the audience. The tourists, Rocky, and the four walls, are offstage when the skit begins. At the appropriate time, the stream, wind, and sun come onstage from the audience.

Once upon a time there was a beautiful beach named Sandy—Sandy Beach. Sandy claimed to be the best foundation there was for a house. As she lay there, tourists stopped and stared at her, admiring the beautiful view. After a while Sandy got tired of their staring and pushed them on their way. She wanted to be appreciated for who she was on the inside.

One day a stud named Rocky walked by Sandy Beach. He was trying to get ideas for a plot for his latest movie. As he walked around Sandy Beach, he was too busy admiring his muscles to notice her. First he flexed his biceps. Then he flexed his triceps. Then his biceps, then his triceps—back and forth he flexed, until he got so confused he lost his step and stumbled into Sandy.

Sandy and Rocky got up on all fours and faced each other, nose to nose. They said in unison, "Who are you?"

Sandy immediately pulled back and sat down with her arms folded. She said, "I'm Sandy Beach. All the best houses get built on me."

Rocky saw that Sandy was very pretty and said, "I can see why!"

Sandy slapped Rocky. Rocky was so mad, he said, "They used to be built on you. Now they're gonna be built on me!" He punched the air a couple of times and flexed his muscles, striking several poses.

As Rocky and Sandy moved to opposite sides of the stage, half the audience cheered for Sandy, and half for Rocky. Rocky whistled, and two walls ran in, joining their hands together over him to form a house.

Sandy whistled, and two guys ran up and asked her if she needed a ride. When they realized she needed a house, they gladly became walls to accommodate her. In fact, they would have done anything for a date with her. When the walls were all in place, Rocky said, "Yo, Sandy—here comes the storm!"

And then the audience rubbed their hands together. They snapped their fingers. Then they slapped their legs. Then they started clapping.

During this crescendo of rain, a stream rose from the audience, heading for the two houses. Sandy Beach grabbed her house and held on for dear life. Sandy's house was more than happy to be held on to. It was a house of love. The stream ran right through Sandy's house, which teetered to one side, but managed to stay standing.

Then the stream headed for Rocky's house. Rocky held his house with one hand and blocked the stream with the other, knocking it to the ground.

Meanwhile, the audience was still slapping their legs. And now a wind ran up, blowing very hard. It arrived at Sandy's house and blew on it with all its might. The wind had such bad breath, Sandy fainted—and the walls toppled to the ground. Then the wind ran over to Rocky and began blowing on his house. Rocky stuck his fist in the wind's stomach, which caused the wind to make gagging and choking noises. Rocky's house exclaimed, "You knocked the wind right out of us!"

But the wind recovered and returned to blow on Rocky again. This time Rocky pulled the wind's finger—and the wind released all of its air and fell to the ground.

The audience continued slapping their legs. They snapped their fingers. They rubbed their hands. Then everyone became silent. The sun came out and went running around the room, spreading light and cheer over everyone.

Rocky looked over at Sandy's toppled house of love and sang the lines from Amy Grant's song: "With me as a firm foundation, you ain't never, never gonna fall."

And so Rocky became the champion foundation—and found a plot for his final film. He's working to get Amy Grant to sing the theme song. ✽

WWF Master of the Universe Heal-O-Rama

Bible text

[1]A few days later, when Jesus again entered Capernaum, the people heard that he had come home. [2]So many gathered that there was no room left, not even outside the door, and he preached the word to them. [3]Some men came, bringing to him a paralytic, carried by four of them. [4]Since they could not get him to Jesus because of the crowd, they made an opening in the roof above Jesus and, after digging through it, lowered the mat the paralyzed man was lying on. [5]When Jesus saw their faith, he said to the paralytic, "Son, your sins are forgiven."

[6]Now some teachers of the law were sitting there, thinking to themselves, [7]"Why does this fellow talk like that? He's blaspheming! Who can forgive sins but God alone?"

[8]Immediately Jesus knew in his spirit that this was what they were thinking in their hearts, and he said to them, "Why are you thinking these things? [9]Which is easier: to say to the paralytic, 'Your sins are forgiven,' or to say, 'Get up, take your mat and walk'? [10]But that you may know that the Son of Man has authority on earth to forgive sins...." He said to the paralytic, [11]"I tell you, get up, take your mat and go home." [12]He got up, took his mat and walked out in full view of them all. This amazed everyone and they praised God, saying, "We have never seen anything like this!"

Cast

❋ Jesus
❋ Teachers of the Law, a.k.a. the Treacherous Two-Faced Twins (2 males)
❋ Friends, a.k.a. the Ferocious Four by Fours (4, males or females)
❋ Paralyzed Person (female)
❋ Audience (seated on floor for best results)

Props

❋ Cape
❋ Mask
❋ Face paint
❋ Pillows stuffed in T-shirts (to increase weight)
❋ Poster board with MEATLOAF written on it
❋ Cardboard circle with ALERT written on it
❋ Ladder, table, etc., to jump down from

Leader hints

If you can, practice beforehand the spectacular belly bashes and knee drops. Professional wrestling (WWF style, at least) is the epitome of melodrama—which makes the craziness of "Heal-O-Rama" utterly appropriate.

Jesus and his opponents, the Treacherous Two-Faced Twins, stand on one side of the stage, waiting to enter the wrestling ring. The paralyzed man and his four friends are on the ladder or table.

It was a hot, sweaty night at the world-famous Roman-occupied Israelidome. The sold-out audience for the WWF Master of the Universe Heal-O-Rama clapped and cheered. It was standing room only, and nobody could even get close to the door. The Heal-O-Rama audience was so excited, it did the wave while singing "The Star-Spangled Banner." *(If the song gets too long, cut it off early by saying something like "The audience went silent because they were awful singers—and besides, so few people actually knew the words.")*

The Master of the Universe Heal-O-Rama was the biggest WWF event to hit Capernaum since the invasion of the Barbarian Babylonian Brothers. After hitting the belly-busting, heavyweight healing circuit around Galilee, the Master of the Universe—Jesus Christ—came back to Capernaum to make meatloaf out of the sumo-sized teachers of the Law *(Jesus enters)*. The crowd went wild!

Jesus motioned his opponents into the ring. Known as the Treacherous Two-Faced Twins, these two guys were mean and ugly—and their breath stank like dead men's bones. To make matters worse, the Two-Faced Twins loved to pick their noses and wipe it on each other.

Jesus Christ, the Master of the Universe, held up his mama's meatloaf recipe and quietly said the Two-Faced Twins, "I'm going to make Jerusalem roadkill outta you."

"Yo! Yo! Yo!" the crowd screamed. The Two-Faced Twins taunted Jesus by making silly faces and sneering "Neener, neener, neener!"

These treacherous, terrible, toenail-painting teachers of the Law weighed a combined total of six-hundred eighty-two pounds and four ounces. The audience shrunk back in fear of these two Torah-twisting terrors. The Two-Faced Twins screamed,

> *We've got the Law, yes we do,*
> *We've got the Law—how 'bout you?*

Then the Two-Faced Twins grabbed one of their fans from the audience *(preferably an adult)*.

"Go, go, go!" cried the audience.

The Two-Faced Twins picked up the fan, spun him around in a circle four times, pulled on his ears, pinned him down, and chest-thumped him five times. Then the Two-Faced Twins danced like ballerinas around the fan's lifeless body. The crowd booed.

The twins pointed to Jesus. "You're next, Galilean geek!" they screamed.

Suddenly, everyone in the Heal-O-Rama ring looked up. Making a spectacular free fall from the Israelidome roof was none other than the famous WWF team, the Ferocious Four-by-Fours, bringing with them a paralyzed person. *(The Four-by-Fours drag or carry the paralyzed girl, and all jump together.)* After their death-defying entrance, they carried the paralyzed person into the ring on their shoulders. The Ferocious Four-by-Fours struck fear into the Two-Faced Twins, who began to shake and convulse.

The Two-Faced Twins began to roll on the ground and cry like babies with diaper rash. The Master of the Universe stepped forward and flexed his biceps. He flexed his tummy in and out. He flexed his cheeks—the ones on his face, that is. The Ferocious Four-by-Fours carried the paralyzed person over to Jesus. But on the way they dropped her.

The paralyzed person pressed her Eternal Life Alert button and cried, "Help! I've fallen and I can't get up!"

Seeing the fantastic faith of the Ferocious Four-by-Fours, Jesus shouted, "How I wish I had more ferocious, fanatical, faith-filled followers!" The Master kneeled next to the paralyzed person. The crowd roared, "Heal her! Heal her! Heal her!"

First the Master of the Universe declared the paralyzed person forgiven of her sins by giving her the Ultimate Bleach Blaster Sin Smasher. The crowd roared again. But suddenly the Two-Faced Twins rushed to Jesus, screaming "Blasphemer!" And they gave Jesus a Neutralizing Noggin Bomb to the head.

The crowd booed.

Jesus quickly recovered and posed a serious question: "Which was easier to say: 'Your sins are forgiven' or 'Get up, take your mat, and walk'?"

The crowd said, "Ooooh!" while the Two-Faced Twins scratched each others heads and then cleaned the dandruff out of their fingernails.

Then, proving that he was the undeniable, authoritative, all-powerful Master of the Universe, Jesus pointed to the paralyzed person and cried, "Pick up your mat and walk!"

Jesus then pointed to the Two-Faced Twins and said, "And you stop picking your noses!"

Slowly, the paralyzed person stood up—and, amazingly, began to dance. The audience went crazy. She started to disco. She grabbed someone from the audience and tangoed. The Ferocious Four-by-Fours grabbed the Two-Faced Twins and pinned them to the ground. The Master stepped on the Two-Faced Twins and raised his arms in victory. He was truly the Master of the Universe.

The audience cheered again, praising God, for they had never seen a Heal-O-Rama as spectacular as this one.

So remember that Jesus has the authority to forgive sins. And also remember that, if you're going to be a WWF tag-team wrestler, make sure your partner is the Master of the Universe. ✻

Seeds and Soils

Bible text

[3]"Listen! A farmer went out to sow his seed. [4]As he was scattering the seed, some fell along the path, and the birds came and ate it up. [5]Some fell on rocky places, where it did not have much soil. It sprang up quickly, because the soil was shallow. [6]But when the sun came up, the plants were scorched, and they withered because they had no root. [7]Other seed fell among thorns, which grew up and choked the plants, so that they did not bear grain. [8]Still other seed fell on good soil. It came up, grew and produced a crop, multiplying thirty, sixty, or even a hundred times."

[9]Then Jesus said, "He who has ears to hear, let him hear."

[10]When he was alone, the Twelve and the others around him asked him about the parables. [11]He told them, "The secret of the kingdom of God has been given to you. But to those on the outside everything is said in parables [12]so that,

"'they may be ever seeing but never perceiving, and ever hearing but never understanding; otherwise they might turn and be forgiven!'"

[13]Then Jesus said to them, "Don't you understand this parable? How then will you understand any parable? [14]The farmer sows the word. [15]Some people are like seed along the path, where the word is sown. As soon as they hear it, Satan comes and takes away the word that was sown in them. [16]Others, like seed sown on rocky places, hear the word and at once receive it with joy. [17]But since they have no root, they last only a short time. When trouble or persecution comes because of the word, they quickly fall away. [18]Still others, like seed sown among thorns, hear the word; [19]but the worries of this life, the deceitfulness of wealth and the desires for other things come in and choke the word, making it unfruitful. [20]Others, like seed sown on good soil, hear the word, accept it, and produce a crop — thirty, sixty or even a hundred times what was sown."

Cast

* Fields (audience)
* Good soil (1)
* Rocky soil (1)
* Thorny soil (1)
* Soil along path (1)
* Seed 1
* Seed 2
* Seed 3
* Seed 4
* Sower (1)
* Throne (1, on all fours)
* Birds (2)

Props

* Signs (4 of them): GOOD SOIL, ROCKY SOIL, THORNY SOIL, SOIL ALONG THE PATH

Leader hints

Involve your whole group (or audience) by dividing them into four groups (for the four soils); give one member in each group their SOIL sign (see props, above). This script works best if you can rehearse a little with the five main characters (the Sower and four seeds). There are several puns in this script; some are just for the reader (who should bear down on the puns with as much corniness as he can muster), and some are supposed slips of the tongue (on *sewing*, *throne*, and *barefoot*), which can get some laughs if the actors are ready for them and begin to act along with the slip before the reader corrects herself.

Once a sower took his needle and thread and began to sew seeds, and—oops! Wrong kind of sowing...

Okay, let's start over. Once a sower—that is, a farmer—planted his seeds. He watched hopefully as the seeds scattered and skipped through the fields, as they made seed noises and looked for places to settle. Wiping the sweat from his brow, the sower watched hopefully, waiting for the seeds to bear fruit. With a loud voice he sat down upon the thorn and—oops, my mistake again. With a loud voice he sat down upon the <u>throne</u> and cheered for his four seeds.

Seed 1 was a healthy, hopeful seed, who danced through the fields, stretched its little arms into a good diving posture, made seed noises, and looked for a place to burrow down into the dirt.

It had been a long journey, and Seed 1 began looking for a place to land. It happened to fall on the soil along the path. Seed 1 whined: "Like, ouch, this soil is totally hard. It's like so pathetic. I am, like, whatever." And it lay uncomfortably on top of the field, twisting and turning and trying to get comfortable. Suddenly birds flapped down toward the seed, did some bird calls to each other, then snatched up the seed and carried it away.

The sower was disappointed and angry. He said, "Man, that soil was for the birds." He started to rise from his throne, but he just stayed seeded. (Stayed seeded? Get it?)

Seed 2 blew all the way to the Avery farm on the opposite side of the room, where it fell on rocky places where there wasn't much soil. The rocky soil looked at Seed 2, and in unison the soil cried, "Yo, Adrian. You're looking pretty good today."

Seed 2 <u>did</u> look promising. It sprung up and began to dance around, pounding its chest and waving its hands in the air like a champion. The sower even stood to his feet and began to sing: "Rocky, my soil, in the bosom of Avery's land" *(to the tune of "Rock-a My Soul")*.

But alas—the rocky soil grew quiet, and Seed 2 got discouraged because no one would root for it. (Get it? Root for it?)

So Seed 2 cried, "Oh, this soil is too shallow." As if that wasn't bad enough, the sower watched as the sun beat down and scorched Seed 2, which quickly withered and died. The sower pounded his hands together, and said, "Curses! Soiled again!"

The thorny soil was only too willing to welcome Seed 3 into it. Yet as soon as Seed 3 got settled down into the thorny soil, things got ugly fast. Thorns reached over and choked the life out of the seed. And as Seed 3 went down, it gasped, "This soil has too many thorns and weeds!" and with that it coughed, gagged, tried unsuccessfully to stand up, then coughed again, then gagged again, then coughed again, gagged, tried to stand again, and finally fell down dead.

Once again the sower had to watch his seed die, never to produce the grain he had been hoping for. His head began to pound with pain as he thought about this tragic waste. "Oh my grain," he groaned. As far as we know, it was the Bible's first recorded "my grain" headache.

Seed 4, however, fell upon good soil—and I mean <u>good</u> soil. It was welcomed, it was embraced, it was patted on the back, it was rubbed on the head, it was given a fifteen-second massage. They even fed the seed a sandwich, which it gobbled up so fast that it made it burp. Boy, was Seed 4 ever grateful that it had fallen here, instead of with some of those other clods. In its most satisfied voice, it said, "Ahhhh, this soil is juuuuuust right!"

It grew up strong and began to go barefoot—oops, I mean, it grew up strong and began to <u>bear fruit</u>, multiplying many times over. *(Face Seed 4 and drill it with multiplication problems; be sure to get answers!)* Five times two. Three times four. Seven times seven. Ten times two. Eight times seven. One thousand seven hundred forty-three times five hundred ninety-six. Just kidding. That was a dirty trick. (Get it? Dirty trick? Seed? Dirt?)

God, you see, sows his seed in our hearts. Depending on our attitude towards God's Word—that is, on what kind of soil is in our hearts—we can bear much fruit, or our name will be mud. ✳

Showdown at Tombstone

Bible text

[1]They went across the lake to the region of the Gerasenes. [2]When Jesus got out of the boat, a man with an evil spirit came from the tombs to meet him. [3]This man lived in the tombs, and no one could bind him any more, not even with a chain. [4]For he had often been chained hand and foot, but he tore the chains apart and broke the irons on his feet. No one was strong enough to subdue him. [5]Night and day among the tombs and in the hills he would cry out and cut himself with stones.

[6]When he saw Jesus from a distance, he ran and fell on his knees in front of him. [7]He shouted at the top of his voice, "What do you want with me, Jesus, Son of the Most High God? Swear to God that you won't torture me!" [8]For Jesus had said to him, "Come out of this man, you evil spirit!"

[9]Then Jesus asked him, "What is your name?"

"My name is Legion," he replied, "for we are many." [10]And he begged Jesus again and again not to send them out of the area.

[11]A large herd of pigs was feeding on the nearby hillside. [12]The demons begged Jesus, "Send us among the pigs; allow us to go into them." [13]He gave them permission, and the evil spirits came out and went into the pigs. The herd, about two thousand in number, rushed down the steep bank into the lake and were drowned.

[14]Those tending the pigs ran off and reported this in the town and countryside, and the people went out to see what had happened. [15]When they came to Jesus, they saw the man who had been possessed by the legion of demons, sitting there, dressed and in his right mind; and they were afraid. [16]Those who had seen it told the people what had happened to the demon-possessed man—and told about the pigs as well. [17]Then the people began to plead with Jesus to leave their region.

[18]As Jesus was getting into the boat, the man who had been demon-possessed begged to go with him. [19]Jesus did not let him, but said, "Go home to your family and tell them how much the Lord has done for you, and how he has had mercy on you." [20]So the man went away and began to tell in the Decapolis how much Jesus had done for him. And all the people were amazed.

Cast

* Tombs (4, males or females)
* Pigs (3, males or females)
* Disciples (4, males or females)
* Chains and irons (2, males or females)
* El Diablo (male)
* Jesus (male)

Props

* White cowboy hat
* Black cowboy hat
* Cowboy boots (for Jesus)
* Round stone
* Jagged stone

Wear a bandanna for this western melodrama, and narrate it with a western twang. Give El Diablo the round stone to put in his hand and the jagged stone to put in his pocket.

As the scene opens...

The tombs are standing onstage.

There once lived a mean hombre named El Diablo. He was possessed by an evil spirit, and he lived in a place called Tombstone. Because he was a bad man, people tried to keep him chained up; they put the chains around his head and his feet. But whenever he flexed his biceps, the chains just fell away. And then he'd let out a cruel and wicked laugh. Even people in the audience took a deep breath of dread.

The man spent his day roaming wild among the tombs: screaming, gasping, yelping, belching, saying "Ouch!" and "Oh, doo doo" over and over again. He sometimes went through this sequence five times without a break.

And sometimes he'd just stop all that, and just howl at the moon—which he did hour after hour, bumping into the tombs and making them topple over. Finally he just collapsed onto the fallen tombstones, where he stopped yelling and only groaned quietly.

And if he was in a really nasty mood, he'd start cutting himself with stones. And because stones aren't the sharpest things in the world, this just seemed to make him angrier. He'd yell repeatedly, "I hate stones, I hate stones, I hate stones." One day, though, he did manage to find one sharp stone. It was his favorite. He even named it Mick Jagged. It was a classic rock.

He used it to cut his arm. Then his face. Then his knees. He tried for that hard-to-lacerate section of his back. But by then, he was totally stoned. So he rolled over, singing loudly, "I can't get no satisfaction."

It was then that Jesus walked onto the scene with his disciples. Jesus wore a white hat and walked bow-legged from many days of walking on water. As he approached the edge of the graveyard, Jesus held up his hand for his disciples behind him to stop. He hollered, "Whoa unto you!"

When they all saw El Diablo laying among the tombs and heard him singing, the disciples yelled, "Yikes!" They grabbed each other and held each other tight. They were plenty scared. They put their hands over each other's ears. After all, El Diablo man was a very poor singer—though the disciples agreed it did sound very much like the original version of the song.

Jesus, on the other hand, walked toward the man as he lay among the tombs. He could see this was a grave situation.

El Diablo shouted at the top of his voice, "What do you want to do with me, Jesus, Son of the Most High God? Swear to me that you won't torture me!"

But when Jesus saw the stones—and especially the bloody "Mick Jagged"—he wasn't about to show sympathy for the devil.

Jesus asked, "What is your name?"

And in a snarly voice, the man hissed, "My name is Legion, for we are meanies"—whoops, I mean many. "We are many."

Anyway, the man grabbed Jesus' boots and begged for mercy and cried like a baby.

The tombs all made fun of Legion, jeering and making snide remarks. They chanted in whiny voices, "Nyah nyah, nyah, nyah, nyah, nyah!" They were happy to see him squirm.

The disciples continued to hold each other and shake in fear.

The man continued to groan, moan, cry, and say, "Oh, doo doo."

Meanwhile, a herd of pigs grazed on the nearby hillside. They munched on grass and made pig-like noises.

Legion interrupted his moaning to plead with a hissing voice, "Send us among the pigs. Allow us to go into them."

Jesus yelled out, "It's a deal—and you'll be hammed for all eternity," and he sent the demons into the pigs.

Then Jesus turned to the disciples and wisecracked, "Well, after all these years of old Legion cruisin' the cosmic mall, he's finally found a porking place."

The disciples giggled and gave each other high fives.

The tombs stopped their chanting, and to the tune of "Amazing Grace" they began to quietly sing the single word "Okay" over and over. The disciples joined in on this Okay Chorale.

El Diablo shook hands with all the disciples and gave Jesus a big ol' Texas hug.

Meanwhile, the demons were really hissed off. The pigs began leaping about frantically, singing old Rolling Stones tunes. Finally, they all ran off and drowned in the sea.

Jesus leaned against one of the tombstones. He was one tired cowpoke. He had been to funerals in his day, but this was quite an undertaking.

Jesus said, "That was some mighty fancy steppin' among those tombstones, pilgrim. What say we give you a new name?"

And from that day on, they called El Diablo the Stone Ranger. And he rode the range in those parts telling everybody how much the Lord had done for him, and how he had experienced God's mercy. ✻

The Wicked Witch of the Beast

Bible text

15On reaching Jerusalem, Jesus entered the temple area and began driving out those who were buying and selling there. He overturned the tables of the money changers and the benches of those selling doves, 16and would not allow anyone to carry merchandise through the temple courts. 17And as he taught them, he said, "Is it not written: 'My house will be called a house of prayer for all nations?' But you have made it 'a den of robbers.'"

18The chief priests and the teachers of the law heard this and began looking for a way to kill him, for they feared him, because the whole crowd was amazed at his teaching.

19When evening came, they went out of the city.

Cast

* Jesus
* Wicked Witch of the Beast
* Lollipop Kids (Peter, James, and John)
* Monkey Changers (4-6, males or females)
* Munchkins (3-4, males or females)

Props

* Empty refrigerator box, or something similar (Yahweh's castle)
* Play money
* Empty bucket (or fill it with shredded paper, if you want)

Leader hints

Take gender liberties if you wish with this skit (as with any in this book): if you want to cast females instead of males in the roles of the Lollipop Kids, replace Peter, James, and John with Petrina, Jamie, and Joan.

As the scene opens...

The Wicked Witch and Munchkins are onstage facing each other.

It was a dark time in the land of Yah. The whole land had fallen under the horrible curse of the Wicked Witch of the Beast. Though Yah had created all the Munchkins, they had stopped following his way.

The Wicked Witch of the Beast had an evil, ear-piercing shriek that made all the Munchkins of Yah tremble. They cowered at her screams—and at her foul breath. They grasped their throats and fell to the floor choking. The people most afraid of the Wicked Witch were the three Lollipop Kids: Peter, James, and John. They had no brains, no heart, and no courage.

The Witch screamed at the Lollipop Kids, "I'll get you, my little pretties! And your little dog Judas, too!"

The Lollipop Kids jumped on top of each other and screamed, "I want my mommy!"

The Wicked Witch of the Beast had set up shop in Yah's castle, the temple. She filled the inside of the temple with cunning, greedy Monkey Changers.

Now the Monkey Changers were a curious lot. They could be found hiding out in the money barrels, under the spell of the Wicked Witch. As a not-too-intelligent group of ATM primates, they were always monkeying around with the Munchkins' money. The Monkey Changers rubbed their greedy little fingers together. They laughed with glee. They rubbed their armpits. They picked fleas from each other's hair. They chanted the Monkey Changer chant:

Ugh, ugh, money, money.

But for the few poor, honest Munchkins who still wanted to worship Yah in the temple, the Monkey Changers charged them big bucks to enter the temple courts. And if the Munchkins dared to protest, the Monkey Changers pummeled them and screamed, "Hear no evil, speak no evil, see no evil." The Monkey Changers may have had wings, but these little devils were no angels.

All the Munchkins sighed at their oppression. The Wicked Witch of the Beast ran around the whole audience and screamed, "You'll never be free, my little wombats!"

Just then a stranger by the name of J.C. appeared in the temple. He was a distant relative of King David, who at one time dated a girl from Kansas named Dorothy—but that's another story.

"Who are you?" cried the Wicked Witch. By way of reply, J.C. slapped the Witch, who fell to the feet of the Lollipop Kids. The Lollipop Kids started to tickle her, and they sang,

We represent the Lollipop Kids, the Lollipop Kids, the Lollipop Kids.

J.C. went over to the Monkey Changer's ATM machine. A Monkey Changer told J.C.: "If you want to deposit, withdraw, or transfer funds, it could be arranged—for a price."

J.C. shouted, 'No moola for me! I'm here to close your account!"

And then J.C. started tearing the place apart. He threw the nearest Monkey Changer onto the Wicked Witch. The Witch cried, "Get off me, gorilla gums!" J.C. grabbed an ATM machine *(this can be merely mimed or improvised)* and threw it onto a Monkey Changer, who happened to be giving the Wicked Witch a wet willy in both ears. The other Monkey Changers were flying around chaotically. J.C. gave them all a King Kong crush to the head. He yelled at them, "Don't you <u>ever</u> make my father's house a den of thieves again!" The audience, amazed, oooohed and aaaahed at J.C.

The Wicked Witch jumped up and tried to seize J.C. The audience screamed, "Lions and tigers and bears—oh my!" But suddenly a marching sound was heard; the audience chanted, "Oh wee oh, oh-weeee oh."

J.C. distracted the Witch by pointing and saying, "Look, I think I see a pair of ruby slippers!" Then J.C. grabbed a bucket of water and dumped it on her head. Later, this act would be known as baptism.

Panicked, the Wicked Witch of the Beast screamed, "Oh no! I'm meeelllting!" And right there in front of J.C., the Wicked Witch vaporized.

The people of Yah were set free from the Wicked Witch and her evil Monkey Changers—set free to worship Yah in the temple.

So remember that God's house is a house of prayer, not a flea market for monkey business. ✻

World Serious: The Empire Strikes Out

Bible text

[1]Jesus, full of the Holy Spirit, returned from the Jordan and was led by the Spirit in the desert, [2] where for forty days he was tempted by the devil. He ate nothing during those days, and at the end of them he was hungry.

[3] The devil said to him, "If you are the Son of God, tell this stone to become bread."

[4]Jesus answered, "It is written: 'Man does not live on bread alone.'"

[5]The devil led him up to a high place and showed him in an instant all the kingdoms of the world. [6] And he said to him, "I will give you all their authority and splendor, for it has been given to me, and I can give it to anyone I want to. [7] So if you worship me, it will all be yours."

[8]Jesus answered, "It is written: 'Worship the Lord your God and serve him only.'"

[9]The devil led him to Jerusalem and had him stand on the highest point of the temple. "If you are the Son of God," he said, "throw yourself down from here. [10]For it is written: 'He will command his angels concerning you to guard you carefully; [11]they will lift you up in their hands, so that you will not strike your foot against a stone.'"

[12]Jesus answered, "It says: 'Do not put the Lord your God to the test.'"

[13]When the devil had finished all this tempting, he left him until an opportune time.

Cast

* Satan (with baseball cap and glove)
* Jesus (with baseball cap and bat)
* Cheering section for Satan (half the audience)
* Cheering section for Jesus (the other half of the audience)

Props

* Baseball caps (2)
* Baseball gloves (1)
* Baseball bat (1)
* Pennants or pom-poms (at least two: one each for Satan's cheering section and Jesus' cheering section)
* Kleenex and ketchup (for bloody nose; optional)
* Chewing gum (Big League brand)

As the scene opens...

Satan is loosening up near the pitcher's mound; Jesus is swinging a bat on deck.

They were cross-town rivals, and at the Skydome was scheduled a life-and-death duel between them: the Prince of Darkness, one of the most famous pitchers ever to take the mound, Satan himself; and the all-star batter, a young kid from Nazareth named Jesus Christ, often referred to as the Illuminator.

Satan stepped to the mound, confident and cocky. He had in his jaw a huge chaw of tobacco, which he spat in the dirt in front of him. He ran his hand along the bill of his cap. Three times he slammed his hand in his glove. He spat again on the ground, and then made several other jock-type adjustments and gestures that we won't describe in a family melodrama. Satan looked across the plate, and scowled at Jesus.

Jesus stepped into the batter's box and just stared back. This stand-off had been going on now for forty days now, a real grudge match. The game had gone into extra innings, and Jesus, full of the Holy Spirit, stood ready at the plate. He flexed his muscles and knocked the mud off his cleats. Then he looked down thoughtfully at that mud, wondering how many humans he could have formed from those tiny lumps of clay. Anyway, he took a few practice swings, and focused on the mound.

The crowd was wild and unruly. They did the wave several times, making lots of noises like wind and rain. It began to get on Jesus' nerves, so he stepped out of the batter's box, waved his hands at the crowd, and told the winds and the wave to be still.

Satan's cheerleaders kept making up stupid cheers, trying to spark a late rally for the Evil One. Three times they yelled:
> *Rip him up, tempt him well,*
> *Come on, Satan—give him hell!*

Then Jesus' cheerleaders yelled back:
> *We may not clap, we may not yell,*
> *But thanks to Jesus, we're not in hell!*

It was quite a scene.

Then Satan went into his windup and threw his first pitch of the inning—a fast ball inside. Satan said, "If you're really the Son of God, command this baseball to turn into bread."

But Jesus just watched it cross the plate, because he knew it was a sucker ball. The pitch was way low. Jesus just looked at the mound, a grim smile on his face, and said, "Folks don't live by bread alone, you know."

Jesus' cheering section went wild. They screamed. They clapped. Three times they chanted,
> *He will, he will rock you.*

That just agitated Satan all the more, out there on the mound. He chewed his gum furiously, he kicked at the dirt on the mound, he glared at everyone in the stadium, even those up in the nosebleed sections—and then he got an idea. He dropped his glove and the ball on the mound, walked to the batter's box, and said to Jesus, real friendly like, "Let's take a walk."

And Satan took Jesus all the way up to the nosebleed section of the grandstands—to the highest point of the Skydome, in fact. But then something embarrassing happened: Satan got a nosebleed. Good thing Jesus was there, because he healed it quickly. Then in his deepest, most macho voice, Jesus said, "Let's play ball!"

"Not so fast," said Satan, wiping his nose. Standing there high above the stadium, Satan motioned to the crowd. "If you worship me, I'll give you everything you see—the crowd, the hot dog stands, even a skybox. All yours."

But even with a pitch like this, Jesus hung tough. He replied, "No way, José. As it says in the Good Book, if you're gonna worship and serve anyone, worship and serve the Lord your God. I mean, what do you take me for anyway, a minor leaguer? I'm already Lord of all these people, I don't like hot dogs, and I have season tickets for the next five centuries to a skybox you wouldn't believe. Now let's get down to the diamond and finish this game."

Satan's cheering section began booing, hissing, shouting, and doing their famous pitchfork chop.

It was oh-and-two—and it was obvious that Satan was getting worried, out there on the mound. But he still had some trick pitches up his sleeve. In slow motion, he went into his windup as he said, "If you're really the Son of God, go back up where we just were—the highest point of the Skydome—and throw yourself down. I mean, of course God will command his angels to catch you and let you down easy."

But Jesus recognized this for what it was: just one more wicked curve. Sure, Satan was right. Angels could do that for him. But that didn't mean that Jesus should take a swing—or a flying leap, for that matter. Instead, Jesus shook off the pitch and said, "Don't you go putting the Lord your God to the test—besides, the Angels are having a bad season."

And then Jesus stuck his tongue out at Satan and said, "Furthermore, Satan, that's three strikes, and you are out."

Yes, folks, it was the first time in baseball history that the batter struck out the pitcher! The crowd went wild. Satan's cheering section cried, "Foul! Foul!" and yelled and stomped their feet. Those cheering for Jesus all held hands with each other, raised their joined hands above their heads, and sang together, "It only takes a park to get a choir going..."

Satan threw down his glove and stormed off the mound. Jesus waved to the crowd and lifted his hands in victory. He didn't run and he didn't make any errors. He was—and is—the undisputed champion. ✽

The Greatest Show on Earth

Bible text

[12]While Jesus was in one of the towns, a man came along who was covered with leprosy. When he saw Jesus, he fell with his face to the ground and begged him, "Lord, if you are willing, you can make me clean."

[13] Jesus reached out his hand and touched the man. "I am willing," he said. "Be clean!" And immediately the leprosy left him.

[14] Then Jesus ordered him, "Don't tell anyone, but go, show yourself to the priest and offer the sacrifices that Moses commanded for your cleansing, as a testimony to them."

[15] Yet the news about him spread all the more, so that crowds of people came to hear him and to be healed of their sicknesses."

Cast

* Jesus, a.k.a. Kingmaster
* Leopard trainer (female)
* Leopards (2-4, all but one of them covered with spots)
* Spot, the circus dog
* Circus audience (the audience)

Props

* Whip and whistle for Kingmaster
* Several sheets of self-adhesive, brightly colored dots or file labels (office supply stores sell them)

Leader hints

Give Jesus several of the self-adhesive dots, so that he can have them in his hands and use them when he heals the leopard.

As the scene opens...

The leopards are down on all fours; all but one has spots. The leopard trainer wields a whip and moves the leopards around the cage. The Kingmaster and Spot are offstage.

It was another incredible performance under the Big Top. The crowd looked up in wonder as the man on the trapeze did amazing feats. They all pointed as he swung to the left. They pointed as he sailed to the right. They oooohed. They aaaahed. They looked straight up with amazement as he swung directly over their heads.

Then they looked down in disgust and wiped their eyes as his sweat dripped into their faces.

In the center ring the leopard trainer was putting the trained leopards through their paces. The leopards growled angrily and ferociously, pacing the ring. The trainer yelled, "Up Simba, up Prancer, up Dancer and Rudolph!" But the leopards just gave her a funny look, and continued growling.

They performed some wonderful tricks. First she had them climb on top of each other and build a pyramid. Then she had them line up, stand up, and put their front legs on the leopard in front of them.

Then the trainer put her head in the mouth of one of the leopards. All the other leopards said in unison, "Oh, that's gross!"

But the crowd loved it. They oooohed. They aaaahed. Then they yelled, "Animal cruelty! Boo! We want Kibbles and Bits!" Kibbles and Bits was a clown act later in the program.

The leopards continued growling and prowling about the cage.

Now what the crowd hadn't noticed until now was one leopard, whose head hung low. Because of a rare skin disease, it didn't have spots like the others. You could tell it was really getting to him, really affecting his inner kitten. In despair—and in some pain—the spotless leopard rolled over in the middle of the cage and lay on its back, paws up.

The crowd oooohed and aaaahed. What a wonderful trick, they thought.

The spotless leopard kicked his legs in the air, half growling and half crying.

The crowd roared with cheers and applause.

But the other leopards knew something was wrong. They stopped their growling, worried about their buddy. Even the leopard trainer came over and began stroking the spotless leopard's head. She stroked its paws. She even offered to put her head inside its mouth.

But the spotless leopard just kept on growling, crying, and kicking.

Suddenly, who should appear in the center ring but the Kingmaster—Jesus himself. He blew his whistle twice—he just loved doing that whenever he entered the ring—then walked over to the ailing leopard and knelt down beside it.

The leopard growled out, "Jesus, Kingmaster, if you are willing you can heal me."

"Are you kidding?" Jesus said. "These spots gotta go!"

Then Jesus rose, blew his whistle twice, and announced in his ringing voice, "Ladieees and gentlemen, booooys and girls—please turn your attention to the center ring as I heal this leopard!"

Then Jesus turned around and yelled, "Here, Spot. C'mere, boy. C'mon, Spot..."

And in ran Spot, the trained circus dog, barking, spinning, wagging his tail, and licking the face of several members of the audience.

Jesus said, "Whoops, wrong spot. Getteth that dog out of here before I turneth him into food for the world's hungry."

Jesus turned to the leopard and gave him spots. Spots began to cover his body. Spots everywhere. And just like that, the leopard was healed.

The crowd oooohed. They aaaahed. The other leopards growled happily. The leopard trainer was so moved she tried to put her head inside Jesus' mouth.

And people all over began to talk about this Kingmaster, and proclaim his work as the Greatest Show on Earth. *

Good Sam, the Levis, and Judas Priest

Bible text

25On one occasion an expert in the law stood up to test Jesus. "Teacher," he asked, "what must I do to inherit eternal life?"

26"What is written in the Law?" he replied. "How do you read it?"

27He answered: "'Love the Lord your God with all your heart and with all your soul and with all your strength and with all your mind'; and, 'Love your neighbor as yourself.'"

28"You have answered correctly," Jesus replied. "Do this and you will live."

29But he wanted to justify himself, so he asked Jesus, "And who is my neighbor?"

30In reply Jesus said: "A man was going down from Jerusalem to Jericho, when he fell into the hands of robbers. They stripped him of his clothes, beat him and went away, leaving him half dead. 31A priest happened to be going down the same road, and when he saw the man, he passed by on the other side. 32So too, a Levite, when he came to the place and saw him, passed by on the other side. 33But a Samaritan, as he traveled, came where the man was; and when he saw him, he took pity on him. 34He went to him and bandaged his wounds, pouring on oil and wine. Then he put the man on his own donkey, took him to an inn and took care of him. 35The next day he took out two silver coins and gave them to the innkeeper. 'Look after him,' he said, 'and when I return, I will reimburse you for any extra expense you may have.'

36"Which of these three do you think was a neighbor to the man who fell into the hands of robbers?"

37The expert in the law replied, "The one who had mercy on him." Jesus told him, "Go and do likewise."

Cast

* Vic Tim (male)
* Thugs (3 males, 3 females)
* Passer-by 1 (male, wearing a pair of Levis)
* Passer-by 2 (female, plugged into her Walkman)
* Good Sam (short for Samantha, female)
* Donkey (big male, on all fours)
* Crowd of pedestrians (audience)

Props

* Walkman radio-cassette player
* Bench (three chairs in a row work fine—or use three people, lined up shoulder-to-shoulder on all fours)
* Bag of play money (actually, anything can be in the bag—it's never opened)

Leader hints

You can either have handy a pair of Levis and a Walkman, or select actors from the audience who already have (or are wearing) these props.

Vic, Passers-by 1 and 2, Sam, and the Donkey are in the back of the room, from where they make their entrances. The six thugs are immediately in front of the first row of the audience, three on the left side, three on the right; in fact, the thugs will launch their ambush from behind the front row.

One day a traveler by the name of Vic Tim was walking up the road to visit his friend Jerry Coe. **(from the back Vic ambles down the center aisle toward the front of the room).** Along the way he was greeted by the pedestrians in the crowd, who shouted, "How's it goin', Vic?" They affectionately patted him on the back and gave him high fives as he walked by. Vic had a smile on his face and a hop in his step.

But when Vic got to the front of the room, a group of thugs came out and blocked Vic's way so he couldn't pass. They said in unison, "We demand to know where you are going and why you are going there!" They repeated this phrase because they didn't get it in unison the first time.

Vic held out a bag of money and said, "I'm off to Jerry Coe's to give him the money I owe him." The thugs looked at each other and said, "What an idiot!" They wrestled Vic to the ground and beat him. Just before Vic lost consciousness he said in a very soft voice, "Help!" The thugs all laughed at him, picked him up, and tossed him on a nearby bench—then took the bag of money and ran off.

About that time, down the road walked a dude, strutting his stuff. He had a new pair of Levis on, and he stopped occasionally to strike a pose. The crowd shouted and whistled as he passed, which only encouraged him to pose more. When he finally got to the front of the room, he saw Vic lying on the bench. He started to kneel to help him, but got up immediately because he got dust on his jeans. He brushed off his pants, and hurried away.

Soon down the road came another walker. She hopped and danced to the beat of her Walkman. As she danced down the road, here and there she pulled pedestrians up to dance with her.

When she got to Vic, she was listening to an oldie by Judas Priest—her favorite song. She closed her eyes and danced wildly around the bench. Vic regained consciousness just enough to reach out and faintly call for help, but she was too busy rocking out to hear him. She danced off the stage, never even noticing him. Vic went unconscious again.

The next one down the road was Good Sam, leading her donkey.

As they passed the crowd, the donkey let out a gigantic "Hee haw!" which scared the pedestrians in the front row off their chairs. Sam being so good and all, she and her donkey helped them back into their seats before continuing their journey.

Then Sam saw Vic. She rushed to the unconscious man, felt for a pulse, couldn't find one, and immediately began to do CPR. She checked again for a pulse. Nothing. Time for mouth-to-mouth resuscitation, Sam thought. Just as her lips were about to meet his, Vic jumped up and said, "I'm all right!"

Sam breathed a huge sigh of relief. The crowd shouted, "Good job, Sam!" The donkey was so excited that he walked over to Vic and started licking him on the face. Vic was so repulsed that he fainted. So Sam put Vic on the donkey, and together they walked offstage to a Motel 6 where Vic could get some rest.

You see, happiness is found in helping others. And we make others even happier if we've first brushed our teeth. ✳

Adventures of the Pro

Bible text

[11]Jesus continued: "There was a man who had two sons. [12]The younger one said to his father, 'Father, give me my share of the estate.' So he divided his property between them.

[13]"Not long after that, the younger son got together all he had, set off for a distant country and there squandered his wealth in wild living. [14]After he had spent everything, there was a severe famine in that whole country, and he began to be in need. [15]So he went and hired himself out to a citizen of that country, who sent him to his fields to feed pigs. [16]He longed to fill his stomach with the pods that the pigs were eating, but no one gave him anything.

[17]"When he came to his senses, he said, 'How many of my father's hired men have food to spare, and here I am starving to death! [18]I will set out and go back to my father and say to him: Father, I have sinned against heaven and against you. [19]I am no longer worthy to be called your son; make me like one of your hired men.' [20]So he got up and went to his father.

"But while he was still a long way off, his father saw him and was filled with compassion for him; he ran to his son, threw his arms around him and kissed him.

[21]"The son said to him, 'Father, I have sinned against heaven and against you. I am no longer worthy to be called your son.'

[22]"But the father said to his servants, 'Quick! Bring the best robe and put it on him. Put a ring on his finger and sandals on his feet. [23]Bring the fattened calf and kill it. Let's have a feast and celebrate. [24]For this son of mine was dead and is alive again; he was lost and is found.' So they began to celebrate.

[25]"Meanwhile, the older son was in the field. When he came near the house, he heard music and dancing. [26]So he called one of the servants and asked him what was going on. [27]'Your brother has come,' he replied, 'and your father has killed the fattened calf because he has him back safe and sound.'

[28]"The older brother became angry and refused to go in. So his father went out and pleaded with him. [29]But he answered his father, 'Look! All these years I've been slaving for you and never disobeyed your orders. Yet you never gave me even a young goat so I could celebrate with my friends. [30]But when this son of yours who has squandered your property with prostitutes comes home, you kill the fattened calf for him!'

[31]"'My son,' the father said, 'you are always with me, and everything I have is yours. [32]But we had to celebrate and be glad, because this brother of yours was dead and is alive again; he was lost and is found.'"

Cast

* Mr. Diggle
* Pro (male)
* Partiers (2 males, 2 females—then 6 others from audience)
* Mr. Sittisun
* Pigs (3-5, males or females)
* Crowd (audience)

Props

* Tennis racket
* Bag of play money
* Grapes (for partiers)
* Wine bottles (filled with water, for partiers)
* Bucket of slop (banana peels, orange rinds, apple cores, whatever)
* Pig noses for the pigs (from novelty or costume shops; optional)

Leader hints

In this melodrama a short chorus is repeated several times by different groups of actors. If the reader gives it a distinctive enough (or goofy enough) rhythm or lilt, the actors can probably mimic it.

As the scene opens...

Pro (holding his tennis racket) and Mr. Diggle stand at the back of the room, from where they make their entrances. Their home is one end of the stage; the road to town extends from their home to the other side of the stage. The first four partiers (two males, two females) enter from stage right. The female partiers hold grapes or wine. Mr. Sittisun with his bucket of slop waits offstage.

Once upon a time lived a man named Diggle, who was known far and wide for his generosity. Everyone loved him, and as he walked through the town people blew him kisses and patted him on the back.

Mr. Diggle had two sons. The younger was a tennis pro, and everyone just called him Pro. He'd walk through town, swinging his racket and striking several tennis poses while everyone ooohed and aaaahed. Actually, he was too big for his tennis shorts.

One day Pro decided he wanted to see the world. He went to his dad and held out his hand. Mr. Diggle slapped him some skin. But Pro shook his head. He didn't want five from his old man—unless it was the five big ones he knew were saved for him. That's right, five thousand dollars. He held out his hand again. Mr Diggle finally got the picture. He walked sadly to the family safe, his shoulders drooping and his feet dragging. He pulled out a bag of money and handed it to Pro.

"Bye-bye!" said Pro to his dad, waving. Then he was out the door and down the road. He got more excited with every step. First he skipped. Then he hopped. Then he jumped. Then he swung his tennis racket. Then he sang a little song about his favorite subject: himself.

> *I'm the Pro, Diggle's son,*
> *I've got my dad's money,*
> *And I'm on the run.*

He chanted it a couple more times, dancing with his tennis racket and swinging his bag of money. Two guys passed him walking the other direction. They had heard Pro say something about money, so they turned and followed him. Two girls passed by, too, and they heard his little jingle about money. So they turned around and joined the group. The four of them began dancing around Pro, singing,

He's the Pro, Diggle's son,
He's got his dad's money,
And he's on the run.

After this performance the crowd went wild, and six people from the crowd jumped up and joined the group. All the guys surrounded Pro, lifted him up, and gave him high fives. All the women surrounded Pro, fed him grapes, and offered him wine. Pro spent money recklessly, even throwing it at those who partied with him.

But then he looked in his bag. It was empty.

One of the people partying with him also realized the money was gone. She whispered it to two others, and they whispered it to two more people, and it spread through the crowd. The guys all left first, saying in unison, "See ya sucker!" They grabbed his racket and left. The women threw the grapes at him and dumped the rest of the wine on his head. Then they laughed and walked away.

Pro wiped wine and squished grapes off his face and sat down. He was alone. He started to cry, making quite a racket. This reminded him of his tennis racket, which made him even more depressed.

Finally he got up and began walking down the road, his shoulders drooping and his feet dragging. He was a sorry sight. A man by the name of Mr. Sittisun was walking by the other way, and he took pity on Pro. Mr. Sittisun took Pro to his own house and gave him the job of slopping the pigs. Pro went out to feed the pigs, and when they saw him they oinked in unison:

He's the Pro, Diggle's son,
He used to have money,
But now he's got none.

Then they snorted and laughed, rolling all over each other in the mud. When Pro put their food in front of them, they knocked each other down to get to the food, which they ate ravenously.

Now Pro hadn't had anything to eat for a while, and he looked at the slop hungrily. He kneeled down and started eating with the pigs.

Suddenly, in a moment of truth, he leapt to his feet. It was time, he knew, to humble himself and head home.

He walked slowly toward his home. Looking up, he saw his dad up on the road ahead, pacing back and forth, rubbing his hands together. He had been there every day since Pro left. When Pro saw him, he froze in his steps. He was just about to turn and run the other way when his dad saw his son, ran up to him, threw his arms around him, and kissed him on the lips. Okay, on the cheek. And Mr. Diggle said,

> *You're the Pro, and you're my son,*
> *Now that you're home*
> *The party's begun!*

The crowd stood up and cheered, and they all came up to welcome him home. They surrounded him, giving him a big group hug.

Pro learned a very big lesson that day. And from that time forward he stuck with his father instead of being stuck on himself. ❄

Pride Comes before a Fall

Bible text

[9]To some who were confident of their own righteousness and looked down on everybody else, Jesus told this parable: [10]"Two men went up to the temple to pray, one a Pharisee and the other a tax collector. [11]The Pharisee stood up and prayed about himself: 'God, I thank you that I am not like other men — robbers, evildoers, adulterers — or even like this tax collector. [12]I fast twice a week and give a tenth of all I get.'

[13]"But the tax collector stood at a distance. He would not even look up to heaven, but beat his breast and said, 'God, have mercy on me, a sinner.'

[14]"I tell you that this man, rather than the other, went home justified before God. For everyone who exalts himself will be humbled, and he who humbles himself will be exalted."

Cast

* Studly stuntman
* Klutzy stuntman
* Pool of Jell-O (3-4, males or females)
* Crocodiles (3-4, males or females)
* Pews (2, both formed by audience members—one in the front row, one in the back—who remain in their chairs and simply allow stuntmen to sit on their laps)

Props

* Mirror
* Hair brush
* Ladder, table, etc., to jump down from

Leader hints

The ladder or table represents a ten-story building. When the stuntmen go to the chapel to pray, stuntman 1 goes to a pew at the front of the room; stuntman 2, to a pew at the back.

As the scene opens...

The pool and crocodiles are center stage.

There once was a studly stuntman who was convinced that he'd never take a serious fall. After all, this slick stuntman had biceps upon triceps. He could run in place faster than any other stuntman. He jumped higher than Superman. This all-powerful stuntman could even do ten push-ups while singing "YMCA" by the Village People. There was nothing this studly stuntman couldn't do. He was confident, brave, famous, successful, and righteous. He never did a stunt wrong.

There was another stuntman, who was very different than the first. This second stuntman was a regular fall guy. He tripped when he walked. His social graces consisted of burping and picking potatoes out of his ears. His hair was a mess from being on fire so many times (which is what happens to a stuntman when he dips himself in gasoline without a flame-retardant suit). He had a limp in his right leg, a left hand that shook, a wiggle in his hips, and a twitch in his face. In a word, he was a klutz.

These two very different stuntmen had at least one thing in common: they both prayed before performing their stunts.

One day both stuntmen were required to jump off a ten-story building into a small pool filled with green Jell-O and crocodiles. The crocs loved to thrash around in the Jell-O and smack their lips. So before the filming began, as was their habit, the stuntmen went to a small chapel near the studio to say their prayers.

The studly stuntman prayed boldly to God: "Lord, thank you for making me a stud." He continued: "Thank you that I am the greatest stuntman in the world." And he ended: "Thank you that I am not like that other crippled rodent of a stuntman behind me." The studly stuntman then pulled out a pocket mirror, brushed his hair, and blew himself a kiss.

The klutzy stuntman just stood in the very back of the chapel and beat his chest ten times with his shaking left hand. He prayed to God only this: "Have mercy on me, God. I keep falling and falling."

Later that day, the klutzy stuntman stood ready to jump from the ten-story building. The pool of green Jell-O jiggled below him. He jumped, had horrendous form on the way down, and did a sickening belly flop into the Jell-O. The crocodiles just stared at him, not bothering to so much as touch him.

The studly stuntman leaped next. His dive was perfect—flawless as usual. He landed in the wading pool of green jello with a big, satisfying SLUURRPP!

Unfortunately, that day just happened to be the day of the Annual Crocodile Cook-off. And the proud, self-righteous stuntman was just what the crocodiles needed to make a perfect humble pie. They seized the studly stuntman, violently ripping him apart limb from limb. The crocodiles looked to the crowd and said, "Mmm, mmm, good."

So be humble before God and don't think you're better than others. You just may have some crocs to deal with. ❋

Zacchaeus the Swinging Sinner

Bible text

[1]Jesus entered Jericho and was passing through. [2]A man was there by the name of Zacchaeus; he was a chief tax collector and was wealthy. [3]He wanted to see who Jesus was, but being a short man he could not, because of the crowd. [4]So he ran ahead and climbed a sycamore-fig tree to see him, since Jesus was coming that way.

[5]When Jesus reached the spot, he looked up and said to him, "Zacchaeus, come down immediately. I must stay at your house today." [6]So he came down at once and welcomed him gladly.

[7]All the people saw this and began to mutter, "He has gone to be the guest of a 'sinner.'"

[8]But Zacchaeus stood up and said to the Lord, "Look, Lord! Here and now I give half of my possessions to the poor, and if I have cheated anybody out of anything, I will pay back four times the amount."

[9]Jesus said to him, "Today salvation has come to this house, because this man, too, is a son of Abraham. [10]For the Son of Man came to seek and to save what was lost."

Cast

* Jesus
* Zacchaeus
* Crowd (4-6, males and females)
* Vines (2 males)
* Ladder (male)
* Tree (male)

Props

* Banana peels

As the scene opens...

Zacchaeus stands by the tree. The tree stands between the two vines, who are holding hands.

Zacchaeus lived in the rough-and-tough jungle village of Jericho. He was the third cousin once removed of Tarzan the ape man. But unlike his stronger, more handsome relative, Zacchaeus was a short, dumpy, conniving little thief, known around the jungle for being a wild swinger who loved hanging out with the local carnivores and parasites. If there was one thing Zacchaeus could do well, it was swinging. He'd swing through the trees every-day, singing *(to the tune of "Singing in the Rain")*:

I'm swinging in the trees, just swinging in the trees.

Unlike most of the jungle inhabitants, Zacchaeus had a lot of money. You see, he worked for the evil owner of the local banana plantation. It was his job to collect the banana tax. It was a slippery business, and everyone hated him for it.

One day while Zacchaeus was swinging in the jungle, a man by the name of Jesus passed through. Jesus was known to be kind and generous—in other words, the very sort of person you could count on to avoid Zacchaeus.

A big crowd gathered around Jesus. Zacchaeus ran around the crowd four times trying to see Jesus. He jumped up and down trying to get a peek. All the other jungle people sneered at Zacchaeus. They threw slimy banana peels at him. They even pushed him to the ground and cried, "Back off, banana slug!"

Zacchaeus had grown used to this abuse. So he came up with a bright idea: he'd do what he did best. Zacchaeus grabbed a vine and began climbing, but the vine broke and he fell to the ground. He grabbed another vine, climbed higher, but that vine broke as well.

Exhausted, Zacchaeus grabbed a ladder and climbed up into an awful-tasting sycamore Fig Newton tree. Just then Jesus and the crowd passed by underneath Zacchaeus. Jesus stopped. The crowd bumped into Jesus, and <u>they</u> stopped.

Jesus looked up at the tree and said, "Hey Zac—how do those Fig Newtons taste?"

"Like wet cardboard. Wanna try one?" Zacchaeus asked.

Jesus shook his head. "No thanks," he said. "I want a real dinner. No more Micky D's Happy Meals. I'm eating at your house tonight."

Zacchaeus was so excited, he smiled and fell out of the fig newton tree. The crowd muttered: "Mutter, mutter, mutter..." Then they grumbled: "Grumble, grumble, grumble..." Then they whined: "Waah, waah, waah..." Why? Because they knew Jesus was going to be the guest of a swinging sinner.

"Wait a minute!" Zacchaeus cried. He told everyone he'd give half of his possessions to the poor. On top of that, he then paid back everyone in the crowd four times the amount he had cheated them. And he had cheated a lot of people.

The crowd yelled, "Ya mon, dis iz goood!"

Jesus was so excited about the change in Zacchaeus's heart, he gave a Tarzan yell. Excited themselves, the crowd began to sing about Jesus, the Lion of Judah:

In the jungle, the mighty jungle, the Lion sleeps tonight.
And everyone rejoiced as Jesus declared that salvation had come to Zacchaeus's tree house.

So the Son of Man came to save those who are lost—which means that if you're going to be a swinger, swing from Jesus' family tree. ✸

Legend of the Blind Man

Bible text

¹As he went along, he saw a man blind from birth. ²His disciples asked him, "Rabbi, who sinned, this man or his parents, that he was born blind?"

³"Neither this man nor his parents sinned," said Jesus, "but this happened so that the work of God might be displayed in his life. ⁴As long as it is day, we must do the work of him who sent me. Night is coming, when no one can work. ⁵While I am in the world, I am the light of the world."

⁶Having said this, he spit on the ground, made some mud with the saliva, and put it on the man's eyes. ⁷"Go," he told him, "wash in the Pool of Siloam" (this word means Sent). So the man went and washed, and came home seeing.

⁸His neighbors and those who had formerly seen him begging asked, "Isn't this the same man who used to sit and beg?" ⁹Some claimed that he was.

Others said, "No, he only looks like him."

But he himself insisted, "I am the man."

¹⁰"How then were your eyes opened?" they demanded.

¹¹He replied, "The man they call Jesus made some mud and put it on my eyes. He told me to go to Siloam and wash. So I went and washed, and then I could see."

¹²"Where is this man?" they asked him.

"I don't know," he said.

¹³They brought to the Pharisees the man who had been blind. ¹⁴Now the day on which Jesus had made the mud and opened the man's eyes was a Sabbath. ¹⁵Therefore the Pharisees also asked him how he had received his sight. "He put mud on my eyes," the man replied, "and I washed, and now I see."

¹⁶Some of the Pharisees said, "This man is not from God, for he does not keep the Sabbath."

But others asked, "How can a sinner do such miraculous signs?" So they were divided.

¹⁷Finally they turned again to the blind man, "What have you to say about him? It was your eyes he opened."

The man replied, "He is a prophet."

¹⁸The Jews still did not believe that he had been blind and had received his sight until they sent for the man's parents. ¹⁹"Is this your son?" they asked. "Is this the one you say was born blind? How is it that now he can see?"

²⁰"We know he is our son," the parents answered, "and we know he was born blind. ²¹But how he can see now, or who opened his eyes, we don't know. Ask him. He is of age; he will speak for himself." ²²His parents said this because they were afraid of the Jews, for already the Jews had decided that anyone who acknowledged that Jesus was the Christ would be put out of the synagogue. ²³That was why his parents said, "He is of age; ask him."

²⁴A second time they summoned the man who had been blind. "Give glory to God," they said. "We know this man is a sinner."

²⁵He replied, "Whether he is a sinner or not, I don't know. One thing I do know. I was blind but now I see!"

²⁶Then they asked him, "What did he do to you? How did he open your eyes?"

²⁷He answered, "I have told you already and you did not listen. Why do you want to hear it again? Do

you want to become his disciples, too?"

28Then they hurled insults at him and said, "You are this fellow's disciple! We are disciples of Moses! 29We know that God spoke to Moses, but as for this fellow, we don't even know where he comes from."

30The man answered, "Now that is remarkable! You don't know where he comes from, yet he opened my eyes. 31We know that God does not listen to sinners. He listens to the godly man who does his will. 32Nobody has ever heard of opening the eyes of a man born blind. 33If this man were not from God, he could do nothing."

34To this they replied, "You were steeped in sin at birth; how dare you lecture us!" And they threw him out.

35Jesus heard that they had thrown him out, and when he found him, he said, "Do you believe in the Son of Man?"

36"Who is he, sir?" the man asked. "Tell me so that I may believe in him."

37Jesus said, "You have now seen him; in fact, he is the one speaking with you."

38Then the man said, "Lord, I believe," and he worshiped him.

39Jesus said, "For judgment I have come into this world, so that the blind will see and those who see will become blind."

40Some Pharisees who were with him heard him say this and asked, "What? Are we blind too?"

41Jesus said, "If you were blind, you would not be guilty of sin; but now that you claim you can see, your guilt remains.

Cast

* Blind man
* Faith healer
* Jesus
* Hypnotist (female)
* Disciples (3, a pair of males and a female)
* Infomercial salesman (must be able to adlib)
* Chair

Props

* Tennis balls (3)
* Spray bottle or bucket of water
* Sunglasses
* Watch
* Stickers (all different shapes and sizes)
* Elastic headband

Leader hints

Spur the audience to participate as the plot unfolds—not only can they throw (harmless) stuff at the blind man when the script calls for it, but, say, when he performs poorly. Remember to give the right props to the right characters so they have them when they come onstage.

As the scene opens...

The blind man sits in a chair onstage.

Back when Jesus lived on earth, a blind man sat every day by the temple gates, earning his living by begging. On this particular day, he sensed an audience was before him—so he really put on a show. He juggled. He slipped on his dark glasses and sang Stevie

Wonder songs. He attempted bizarre contortion tricks, like putting both feet behind his head. But when he heard no money coming his way, he got desperate and simply cried out for money, food, or anything else people would give him. "Dude, I'm blind, help me out," he said.

At that, several people in the audience did respond, tossing him small change, shoes, gum wrappers, anything else they could find in their pockets.

But what the man <u>really</u> yearned for was his sight.

He tried everything in hopes of being able to see again. He tried a faith healer, who screamed in an exaggerated Southern accent, "I demand all forces of evil to flee your eyes—I said, *eyeeees*!" The healer massaged the blind man's temples, slapped him on the forehead, and yelled, "Be heeeeeaaled!" The blind man fell over from the force of the blow, but received nothing more than a headache and a potent whiff of the healer's bad breath.

The blind man tried a hypnotist, who dangled a watch in front of his eyes. The hypnotist said, "You're getting sleepy, veeerrry sleeeepy..." *(the narrator dozes off)*...Oh, sorry 'bout that...uh, where was I?...oh, yeah. The problem was watching that dangling watch swing back and forth. The blind man just couldn't keep his eyes on it. So after several tries, the hypnotist gave up, but left the blind man some chemical patches *(these are the stickers)*, instructing him to wear them on his face to release sight-enhancing chemicals through the skin. The blind man immediately placed several patches on his face—so many, in fact, that he began to hallucinate from the smell of glue on the stickers.

Next he went to the marketplace to see—okay, to <u>hear</u>—an infomercial for Eye-Master. The salesman was famous for his healing products. Just a few weeks earlier the blind man's crippled friend was healed, thanks to this same salesman's Thigh-Master. The salesman made a passionate pitch for the miraculous Eye-Master *(here the salesman ad libs a sales pitch, with the headband as the Eye-Master)*. Convinced that this was the right product for him, the blind man bought one. But this didn't cure his blindness, either.

Then one day Jesus and his disciples stopped in front of the blind man. The disciples speculated about why he was born with such an unfortunate handicap.

"I think it's his parents' fault," one disciple said. "I think they refilled a Taco Bell soda cup without paying, and God was punishing their sin by making their son blind.

Another disciple said, "I think he wiggled too much while in his mother's womb, and his eyes rubbed up against her spine."

Then Jesus spoke up and explained that this blindness was not a result of any particular sin, but that it simply was an opportunity to display the work of God in the man's life.

Jesus said, "While I am in the world, I am the light of the world." Then he spit. He aimed for the ground, but it hit the leg of one of the people in the audience. Jesus tried again, and this time managed to hack up this big loogy and let it fly right there on the ground in front of him. Then Jesus put his fingers into the spit, rolled a small mud ball, then actually rubbed this nasty concoction on the blind man's eyes.

As you can imagine, the blind man was disgusted and screamed obscenities at the crowd around him, like "Sick! Gross! I'm gonna puke!"

Jesus told his disciples to wash out the man's eyes by pouring water over his head. When that was done, the blind man said, "Thanks. I needed that. Hey...what th—...I feel different...kinda fresh and alive..."

And then the man realized what it was—he could see! Shapes and colors unfolded before him! Caught up in the ecstasy of the moment, he fluttered around the room like a ballerina. He touched everything in sight. He stroked one person's cheek, ran his fingers through another's hair, stared wistfully into the eyes of another.

He turned to Jesus and said, "Whoever you are, thanks a million. Gotta go now—things to do, people to see. You know how it is."

"I sure do," said Jesus. And with that, the man turned to run off-stage—but tripped over his chair. The crowd gave the chair a big round of applause. *

Youth Specialties Titles

Professional Resources
Developing Spiritual Growth in Junior High Students
Developing Student Leaders
Equipped to Serve: Volunteer Youth Worker Training Course
Help! I'm a Sunday School Teacher!
Help! I'm a Volunteer Youth Worker!
How to Expand Your Youth Ministry
How to Recruit and Train Volunteer Youth Workers
The Ministry of Nurture
One Kid at a Time
Peer Counseling in Youth Groups
Advanced Peer Counseling in Youth Groups

Discussion Starter Resources
Get 'Em Talking
4th-6th Grade TalkSheets
High School TalkSheets
Junior High TalkSheets
High School TalkSheets: Psalms and Proverbs
Junior High TalkSheets: Psalms and Proverbs
More High School TalkSheets
More Junior High TalkSheets
Parent Ministry TalkSheets
What If...? Provocative Questions to Get Teenagers Talking, Thinking, Doing
Would You Rather...? 465 Questions to Get Kids Talking

Ideas Library
Combos: 1-4, 5-8, 9-12, 13-16, 17-20, 21-24, 25-28, 29-32, 33-36, 37-40, 41-44, 45-48, 49-52
Singles: 53, 54, 55
Ideas Index

Youth Ministry Programming
Compassionate Kids: Practical Ways to Involve Kids in Mission and Service
Creative Bible Lessons in John: Encounters with Jesus
Creative Bible Lessons on the Life of Christ
Creative Programming Ideas for Junior High Ministry
Creative Socials and Special Events
Dramatic Pauses
Facing Your Future

Great Fundraising Ideas for Youth Groups
Great Retreats for Youth Groups
Greatest Skits on Earth
Greatest Skits on Earth, Vol. 2
Hot Illustrations for Youth Talks
Memory Makers
More Hot Illustrations for Youth Talks
Hot Talks
Incredible Questionnaires for Youth Ministry
Junior High Game Nights
More Junior High Game Nights
Play It! Great Games for Groups
Play It Again! More Great Games for Groups
Road Trip
Super Sketches for Youth Ministry
Teaching the Bible Creatively
Up Close and Personal: How to Build Community in Your Youth Group

Clip Art
ArtSource Vol. 1—Fantastic Activities
ArtSource Vol. 2—Borders, Symbols, Holidays, and Attention Getters
ArtSource Vol. 3—Sports
ArtSource Vol. 4—Phrases and Verses
ArtSource Vol. 5—Amazing Oddities and Appalling Images
ArtSource Vol. 6—Spiritual Topics
ArtSource Vol. 7—Variety Pack

Videos
Edge TV
God Views
The Heart of Youth Ministry: A Morning with Mike Yaconelli
Next Time I Fall in Love Video Curriculum
Promo Spots for Junior High Game Nights
Understanding Your Teenager Video Curriculum

Student Books
Grow For It Journal
Grow For It Journal through the Scriptures
Next Time I Fall in Love
Wild Truth Journal for Junior Highers
101 Things to Do during a Dull Sermon

259.2304
F461

LINCOLN CHRISTIAN COLLEGE AND SEMINARY

90970

3 4711 00091 3196